William Prentice was him... ...up in a shop from early childhood, and most of his close relatives either owned or worked for small businesses. Much of his own career followed a different path and, after graduating as a chemist, he spent nearly thirty years in the international oil industry. He has worked and travelled in many countries and has been involved in starting up many new projects. Ten years ago he left to start his own business as a management consultant and freelance writer.

Working for Yourself

WILLIAM PRENTICE

How to Start a
Successful Business

PANTHER
Granada Publishing

Panther Books
Granada Publishing Ltd
8 Grafton Street, London W1X 3LA

First published in Great Britain by
Panther Books 1980
Revised edition published 1984
Reprinted 1985

ISBN 0-583-13125-5

Printed and bound in Great Britain by
Collins, Glasgow

Set in Times

TO
SHEENA and JIMMY
who started it

Contents

Foreword

'After many years of neglect, small businesses are at last being allowed to "come in from the cold". The truth has penetrated that unless small businesses are encouraged to start and prosper, there will be no new industries to provide jobs for the people cast off from dying industries. As the initiator of the Industrial Revolution, Britain has far too many of the latter. More important still, unless these new firms succeed, there will not be enough jobs for the new employees, the young people who come out each year from the educational system.'

With the above words, I opened the Foreword to the first edition of this book. Since then, the number of unemployed has doubled and is just beginning to show some signs of levelling off. As predicted, unemployment has fallen most heavily upon the manufacturing sector and upon school-leavers.

The only consolation arising from this tragedy is that it has hastened the realization that the economic future of Britain depends upon the 'job creators' – and if a country has no economic future it has no future of any other kind. All the main political parties now accept the need to foster the growth of small businesses. It has at last sunk in that not only do small businesses already provide one-third of all the jobs in the wealth-creating sector, but they provide the best prospects for future expansion of employment.

The present government has taken a number of steps to cope with the unemployment problem. Some of them are cosmetic measures to reduce the number of people on the unemployed register, but other schemes do help small businesses, either directly or indirectly. The scope of these schemes and how to find out more about them are discussed in the appropriate chapters of this book.

In the four years since this book was first published, not only the government has jumped on the small-business bandwagon. Local authorities have developed schemes for encouraging new enterprises in their own districts. Large firms (e.g. British Steel, Shell) have provided accommodation at attractive rents to small new enterprises. In many parts of the country, local organizations and local branches of national organizations have shown great initiative in developing ways of smoothing the path of would-be entrepreneurs.

New business stories are common in the national and local newspapers, many of which now have regular small-business features. Radio and television now regard entrepreneurs as newsworthy, and from time to time present courses aimed at helping those starting a new business. The small-business owner has become something of a folk-hero, and as Britain cautiously emerges from the worst recession for 50 years, the would-be entrepreneur has never had it so good.

Much of the publicity given to the experiences of those starting a business today is refreshingly realistic. Gone are the glamorous tales of the Horatio Alger type, when the entrepreneur hero could do no wrong and success automatically crowned his efforts. Today's stories deal with failure as much as success, and today's entrepreneurs are much less starry-eyed. They know that there are many pitfalls and they want to know how to avoid them in *their* business. It is for these readers that this book is written.

The help which can be provided by a comprehensive, up-to-date book is unique. A book can be read – and re-read – and the reader can stop to reflect upon what is written, to consider how it is confirmed (or otherwise) by personal experience, and to study how it relates to his or her particular interests. You can also keep a book beside you for instant future reference. On the other hand, once a book is set in type, its contents are 'frozen'. Therefore I have devoted much effort to explaining how to get current information on *your* business and *your* location.

In preparing this revised edition, every care has been taken to get the facts up-to-date and correct, but I am only human and may have made mistakes. Moreover, the small-business scene is changing rapidly, and what is correct when written may be wrong when it is read. Advice which is sound in general may not apply in a particular instance. Recommendation of specific services is given in good faith, based on my own experience and that of others, but the aims of organizations change and so do the people who run them. For all these reasons, no legal liability can be accepted for the advice given in this book. You must check with your own professional advisers that it is valid in *your* case.

As the examples in the text show, I fully appreciate that many new businesses are started by women. Consequently, although I have used 'he', 'him' or 'his' in many places to avoid clumsy writing, these should be read as 'she' or 'her' when appropriate to do so.

This book is addressed to all those who have the abilities and the desire to start a business. My object is to provide encouragement and hope – and the knowledge which will help to make YOUR business successful.

Stansted Mountfitchet   *William Prentice*
                                          December 1983

Part I: Choosing Your Business

CHAPTER 1

What Can You Offer?

Starting a business will not, in itself, solve any problems, whether national or personal. These will only be solved if the business you start is successful. To start a successful business you must meet three conditions: (1) that you possess or acquire certain abilities; (2) that you choose the right business to start; (3) that you go about starting it in the right way. The fact that you are reading this book shows that you want *your* business to succeed. I too want *your* business to succeed: that's why I wrote it.

This chapter will help you to assess *your* present abilities and show where these need to be strengthened. The next three chapters present a systematic method for choosing the business which best suits *your* interests and abilities. The rest of the book explains how to start *your* business in the way most likely to achieve success.

Why start a business?

More people are becoming attracted by the idea of starting a business these days. After all, being your own boss offers you the freedom to choose work you really enjoy and to work where, when and how you like. It also offers the prospects of enjoying a greater share of the fruits of your efforts.

On the other hand, added freedom is accompanied by added responsibilities. No one guarantees your income, finds work for you to do or pays you when you are sick. No one provides the hundred and one support services that are taken for granted in an established enterprise: typing, filing, canteens, cleaning, etc. In addition, if things go wrong, you have no one to blame but yourself.

Starting a business means taking a risk. Why then are so many not only willing but eager to accept the challenge? The popular belief is that people start a business because 'you can make more money working for yourself than working for someone else'. Is it really as simple as that? Several recent studies have thrown a little more light on this subject – what psychologists call the *motivation*.

It has been found that, although the desire to make more money is important, it is not the only motive nor even, for many, the most important one. Some start a business because they believe they could run one better than their present employer does; they want to prove it. Others desire to make new products, use new methods or invent new processes, but they cannot persuade their present employer to apply their ideas.

Still others experience a rethinking of what they want to do with their lives and, having decided this, cannot find a job which allows them to do it. But the most important motive of all which emerges from these studies is a *desire for independence*.

Qualities for success

The first and most critical quality is the one we have just mentioned. *Motivation* provides the driving force needed to overcome the difficulties you will inevitably meet if you start your own business. Many problems beset the entrepreneur: money, customers, staff, rules and regulations, supplies, somewhere to work, even just plain weariness. Unless you have a strong will to succeed, you will give up.

Each different kind of business has of course its own pattern of requirements but there are a number of general qualities which the entrepreneur must possess to at least some extent to provide a reasonable chance of success in any business. The principal ones are given below but not in any order of importance, since this depends upon the business chosen.

Business acumen is a rather general term which embraces a number of activities, e.g. buying, selling, negotiating terms, clinching a deal, etc. Some few are gifted with an outstanding flair while others, seemingly, will never learn. Most people, however, can improve their level of skill by study and practice.

Figure sense is the ability to perform simple arithmetic with reasonable accuracy, combined with sufficient 'feeling' for figures to detect on sight when there is a gross error in a calculation.

Word sense is the ability to express oneself clearly in speech and to understand equally clearly what others are saying. Allied to this, although the level of skill may be different, is the ability to write and understand business correspondence.

Emotional stability is required to a greater or lesser extent in all businesses, since the owner is subject to a wider range of provocations than the average employee.

Good health tends to be taken for granted by those who have it but its importance should not be overlooked. Not only does income drop sharply when the entrepreneur is sick but a major deal can be jeopardized by even a short illness at a critical moment.

Physical and mental energy are needed to sustain you during these occasions, which seem to arise during the early days of all businesses, when it is necessary to work long hours for extended periods.

Self-assessment

Before you start your business, before you even decide what kind of business to start, you must take a good look at yourself. What are you good at – the *strengths* you want to exploit in your business? What are you not good at – the *weaknesses* you must overcome – or protect by choosing a business where they don't matter?

To help you in your self-assessment, a number of questions are posed below for you – the reader – to answer. You must try to answer these as honestly as possible since, if you don't, you may find you are not making the best use of your strengths and/or exposing your weaknesses.

Not only must you be honest with yourself, you must also be realistic. If you undertake things you cannot really do, you simply build up trouble for yourself. You will find yourself hopping from one crisis to another, leaving a trail of dissatisfied customers behind you and earning a reputation for unreliability – someone who promises but can't deliver.

Nor should you veer to the other extreme. There is no place in business for false modesty. By working well within your capacity all the time, you may avoid becoming over-stretched but you restrict yourself to the easier and less interesting tasks. You will probably also restrict your income since, generally speaking, the easier a job the less it is paid. If you underestimate your talents, you condemn yourself to getting less money and less fun out of your business.

Write down the answer to each of the following questions, because somehow it is harder to kid oneself in writing. What can sound quite convincing when said emphatically with a lot of arm-waving, looks what it is when written down – rubbish! Another reason is that we shall make use of these answers in other chapters of this book. If the answers are written down, it saves you having to think them afresh each time.

Q.1 Can you control money?
Do you keep an accurate check on your current account so that you always know how much you have in it? Do you keep a household budget? Do you find that holidays cost

roughly what you expected? Do you keep money in reserve in case of unexpected bills or bargain opportunities? Do you save up ahead of major expenditures or do you rely on HP or credit? Do you get the best interest rate on your savings?

Q.2 Can you buy?

Do you compare prices in different shops before buying? Do you decide on price alone or do you consider quality, reliability, running cost, ease of repair, etc.? Do you belong to Consumers' Association? Do you buy many things on impulse? Do you find out the experiences of other people who have one before you buy something? Are you often 'sold a pup'?

Q.3 Can you sell?

Do you have any experience of selling from your present or previous jobs? Have you ever sold anything by advertising in the local paper? Did you get the price you expected? If you ever collect for local charities, do you raise more or less than other collectors? Do you get a good trade-in price for your old car when you buy another? Have you ever run a stall in a jumble sale or bazaar?

Q.4 Do you preserve your property?

How well do you look after your house, furniture, car, clothes, domestic appliances? Do you do many of your own repairs? Do you service things regularly or wait until they break down? Do you have a lot of breakdowns? Do you find things seem to last a long time? Do you do your own home decorating?

Q.5 Do you get on with other people?

Do you find it hard to approach strangers? Are you invited to many parties? Do your friends wait for you to invite them to your home or do they drop in casually? Have you made any new friends in the past year? Do you chat to people you meet in shops, restaurants or buses? Do your hobbies involve other people (e.g. dancing, football) or are they solitary (e.g. gardening, fishing)?

Q.6 Can you influence other people?
Do you usually go along with what other people want to do? Do you often persuade others to 'be reasonable, do it my way'? In your family, who decides where you go on holiday? Can you often persuade your boss to accept your ideas at work? Do you have much difficulty in handling your assistants? Are you on any club or society committees? How much attention do other members pay to your ideas?

Q.7 Can you organize?
Has your work given you any organizing experience? Have you ever been on any committees? Have you ever organized a political event (e.g. meeting, canvassing, fund-raising)? Have you ever organized a social event (e.g. dance, whist drive, concert)? Have you ever organized a sporting event or outing? Do you normally plan the family holidays? How successful are the things you organize?

Q.8 Can you figure?
How often do you make mistakes in simple arithmetic? Can you understand your payslip (when you try)? Have you ever been treasurer of a local society? Can you work a pocket calculator? Are you able to check your PAYE coding? Do you have any difficulties in coping with the conversion to metric? Can you tell at a glance whether a VAT calculation is roughly correct? Are bills in restaurants usually about what you expect?

Q.9 Can you write a good letter?
Do you have much experience in writing business letters? Do you write many personal letters? Do you have much difficulty in understanding letters from government departments and local councils? Can you type? Have you a dic-

tionary at home? Do you read any 'quality' newspapers? Do you read many books? Do you ever find that people don't understand your letters? Do you write in a style which is very different from how you speak?

Q.10 Can you listen?
Can you listen to someone for very long without interrupting? Are many of the people you meet rather boring? Do you ever wonder if you yourself might be thought boring? Do you often hear people use words you don't understand? Have you much difficulty in understanding people with a strong local dialect or foreign accent? Do you easily become flustered when several people speak at once? Do you learn more easily by reading about something or by listening to someone explain it?

Q.11 Do you have ups and downs?
Do you often have days when you feel on top of the world? Do you often have days when you are in the depths of despair? Do you keep in much the same frame of mind all the time? Do you have to be in the mood to do certain tasks? Do you like people at some times and dislike them at others? Are you easily upset by events or the behaviour of other people? Can you talk yourself out of black moods?

Q.12 Do you have good self-control?
Do you lose your temper easily? Do you cool down again quickly? What causes you to get steamed up? Have you ever struck anyone? Are you able to avoid situations where you might lose your temper? Do you ever sulk? Can you suffer fools without showing your suffering?

Q.13 Are you fit?
Taking into account your age and physique, are you fitter than average? How often do you have colds or 'flu? Have you ever had a serious illness? Do you suffer from any

chronic ailment? Does it affect your work performance? Is your eyesight good (with glasses if worn)? Is your hearing good? Can you lift heavy weights? Can you work long hours without becoming exhausted? How many days have you been absent from work through sickness in the last three years? Do you take any regular exercise?

Q.14 Are you a self-starter?

Do you like to know exactly what you have to do and how to do it? Do you have a lot of supervision in your present job? Is your working speed fixed by others or have you much scope to vary your output? Is your pay related to output? Do you look for ways of improving how you do your job? Do you often have ideas about improving methods of doing other people's jobs? What do you do if you have no work to do – wait for the boss to tell you?

Q.15 Will you get support?

Is your family behind you in your venture? Do they think your idea is good? Have they confidence in your ability to succeed? Are they able and willing to give you financial help? Will they do jobs for you if necessary? Is your wife/husband willing to accept a changed domestic routine and a greater share of the chores? Is she/he willing to accept cuts in domestic expenditure? Have you any friends who will give moral, financial or practical support?

In answering the foregoing questions, do not rush to put down the first thing which comes into your head. Think about each one in turn. Once you have answered the questions in detail, give yourself an overall rating on each of the fifteen main questions, scoring 1 for a 'very low' rating, 2 for 'fairly low', 3 for 'average', 4 for 'fairly high' and 5 for 'very high'.

There is no 'right' and 'wrong' answer to these questions, except in the sense that there is an honest, realistic answer which applies to YOU. The object of the exercise is to reveal where you are strong and where you are weak. The purpose of this is to guide you when choosing your business so that you can exploit your strengths and avoid exposing your weaknesses. A secondary purpose is to spot those weaknesses which you may be able to overcome by study, training or additional experience.

If your total score is about 45, then you rate about average overall. But careful selection of a business to fit your pattern of strengths and weaknesses can give you an above-average chance of success.

If your total score is about 25 or lower, you should ask yourself whether you are being unduly modest. Look again at your answers and re-rate yourself. If you still come out with a low score, you have probably a less than average chance of making a success of your business. You will certainly need to be highly selective in choosing it, since you have few areas of strength to exploit and many areas of weakness to shield.

If your total score is about 65 or more, your self-honesty and realism are suspect, since few such paragons exist, even among highly successful men of business. As a rule, the latter have become highly successful, not because of excessive personal endowments but through very clever choice of how to use what gifts they have. So look at your answers again and rate yourself more strictly.

CHAPTER 2

What the Business Needs

You will not be equally successful in every type of business. Just as each person has his or her own unique pattern of abilities, so has each business its own particular pattern of requirements. Some understanding of how these needs vary with the nature of the business helps you to see how some businesses will suit you better than others. Obviously the closer the match between what the business needs and what you can offer, the greater your chance of success.

Broadly speaking, there are three main types of business activity: making things, selling things, providing a service. In practice, the boundaries between these may be hard to define and many businesses display elements of all three. Nevertheless, in most businesses – and particularly in small businesses – one type of activity predominates. This gives a clue to the personal qualities and experience needed by the owner of such a business. The purpose of this chapter is to discuss the requirements of different types of business, to help you decide 'that's the one for me'.

Making things

Reflect for a moment on the great number of different things you look at, use or consume in the course of just one day. In today's society, few of us are self-sufficient – nearly all these things have been produced by someone else. This gives you some idea of the variety of products provided by businesses which make things. But it does not stop there. These businesses themselves use or consume many more things. So too do other types of business . . . and national, regional and local authorities . . . and public corporations . . . and so on.

The bewildering variety of products is mirrored by an almost equally bewildering variety of businesses, all busy making things. Nevertheless, one can pick out certain features common to all or nearly all manufacturing businesses.

First, they need a *workplace*, because products have to be made somewhere. Second, they need *equipment* for the process of making. To shelter the people engaged in manufacture, and their equipment, the process is usually carried out inside a building. Unless you already possess one, you will have to buy or rent a workplace. Hence, to provide a workplace and equipment, manufacturing businesses usually need some *fixed capital*.

Supplies of materials or components are needed from which the product is made. Frequently these – and the wages of the 'makers' – have to be paid before the customer pays for the product, which necessitates some *working capital*.

Making things usually demands *knowledge* and *skill* – knowledge of the material worked upon and the use to which the product is put, skill in carrying out the making process and in looking after the equipment. To keep the knowledge and skill requirements within reasonable bounds, and to make efficient use of the equipment installed, it is necessary to limit the range of products made. This applies even to those businesses making a succession of unique articles.

Selling things

Although the variety of things sold is just as great as that of things made, the range of articles handled in a selling business tends to be greater than that in a making business. On the other hand, the number of different ways of selling things makes it more difficult to generalize about selling businesses. It is therefore convenient to discuss selling businesses under several main headings.

The best-known type is the *retail shop*, in which goods are displayed so that customers may choose what to buy (or not). There are many variants of the main type (e.g. wholesale warehouses, cash and carry, discount stores) but they all share certain common features. They need premises and a stock of goods for sale, which requires fixed and working capital.

Instead of displaying goods in a shop, some businesses take the goods to the customer by means of a *mobile shop* or *market stall*. Some capital is needed to provide a van and enough goods to stock it but this is much less than is needed for a shop. Such businesses offer greater variety of working location but a less sheltered environment and hence demand a high standard of health.

In *mail order* selling, by contrast, the customer buys without having seen the goods. The entrepreneur 'displays his wares' in pictures and words in press advertising or catalogues. Such businesses may attract those who find difficulty (e.g. through shyness) in face-to-face selling. Working capital is needed for advertising or catalogue printing and distribution. Initially it may be possible to obtain the goods as orders come in but, as the business grows, it becomes necessary to hold stock to ensure prompt fulfilment of orders.

All of the above types of business require some skill in buying and selling. A thorough knowledge of the goods being sold may also be essential for success in some trades. An ability to establish and maintain good relations with suppliers and customers is very important.

Providing a service

Various types of service can be provided. For instance, there are personal services (e.g. hairdresser, stockbroker); services to domestic equipment and premises (e.g. plumber, painter); services to business equipment and premises (e.g. typewriter mechanic, office cleaning). There is, in addition, a wide range of specialist sub-contractors helping firms to cope with fluctuations in workload or demands for special skills which their own staff lack.

Many customers who employ a service do so because it is something they are unable to do for themselves. Consequently, it is essential that anyone starting such a business has the requisite skills and knowledge to perform it effectively. One hears many horror stories about incompetence but businesses which offer inadequate service do not prosper for long. It is also essential that you enjoy making contact with new customers and helping them.

By their very nature, many service businesses do not need a workplace; it is sufficient to have an address and telephone number at which you can be contacted. In addition, the equipment required is often relatively inexpensive. Consequently, service businesses tend to need less capital than those concerned with making or selling. Many can be started from one's home address on a part-time basis. It is hardly surprising, therefore, that a high proportion of people starting a business for the first time choose to do so in the service sector.

Class of market

There is a range of markets possible for any product or service. At what point on the quality scale will you aim – the 'bespoke' luxury product, a range of good-quality products or a cheap mass-produced article? It is usually unwise to attempt to cover the whole field when starting a business, since different product qualities require different production methods and different sales-promotion methods. Product quality also influences the 'image' needed by your business, affecting such things as the design of your stationery and how your workplace is furnished.

Another aspect of the market is the type of customer at whom the product or service is aimed. This may be the general public, commercial firms, local authorities, public corporations or government departments. The choice of customer affects the way your business is organized and the methods of promotion. It also influences the number and type of sales personnel, since the task of selling ten thousand articles to separate users is very different from that of negotiating a contract for ten thousand articles to one customer.

The above decisions regarding class of market are quite fundamental since they affect how you set up your business at the outset. You may feel that you don't care who buys your product – your are happy to sell to anyone. If you feel this way, you have missed the point. *Different qualities of product are made in different ways, from different ingredients or components, and are sold by different methods.*

The very large companies who supply a wide range of products to various types of customer subdivide their activities. They have different production lines for different qualities and a different sales team for each class of market. They may even set up separate subsidiary companies to make and sell under different brand names.

As a beginner, with limited resources, you have to concentrate your efforts. You must decide on what to specialize in. Your choice will be dictated by personal preferences, by your experience and by your resources. For instance, do you get more satisfaction by making a high-quality product or by producing large quantities? Are you happy to pander to luxury customers who can pay for it or do you like to give satisfaction to large numbers of people?

Resources

Different types of business make different demands upon the three main business resources – money, time and people. Money may be needed to buy or rent business premises and fix them up. You may need to get equipment such as machinery, fittings, tools, transport, etc. The total you need for these purposes is your *fixed capital*, so called because once spent this money cannot quickly be recovered and usually not without some financial loss.

You will also need *working capital* to cover initial stocks of raw materials or goods for sale and to bridge the time lag between expenditure and income. In a new business you often have to pay cash on the nail for supplies (and of course for wages) but may wait months for customers to pay you. It is also prudent to allow for the fact that you are quite likely to be running at a loss in the beginning.

The second resource is time – *your time*. Is the venture full-time? If so, does full-time mean five 8-hour days or seven 16-hour days per week? Does part-time mean several full days per week or a few hours every day? How will you cope with sickness and holidays? Some businesses require flexibility in working hours to cope with seasonal trade, emergency service or an unforeseen 'jumbo' order.

The third resource is *people*. How many people do you need to run the business on the scale you envisage and what skills must they have? Are such people available locally or must you train them? Have you any idea what wages to pay them? If you lose the initial staff or get an opportunity to expand, can you get more staff quickly?

If the demands of the business don't quite match the re-sources available, you may be able to achieve some inter-change between resources. With more money, you can hire extra staff to save your time. If you work longer hours, you may need fewer staff and save money. If that doesn't work, you can perhaps change the range or scope of your project. Can you buy in more (or fewer) semi-finished components? Can you put out more (or less) work to contract?

Management

A popular definition of management is 'the art of getting things done through people'. In this sense, the owner of almost any business has some management responsibilities. In addition to general management, there are specialized branches of management, of which the most common are: operations, marketing, finance, personnel and administration. There is also a host of other, still more specialized branches of management, which may be very important in specific businesses.

Operations management is often called production or works management in a manufacturing setting. This branch is concerned with making the product or providing the service that the customer wants. It is very much engaged in the 'nuts and bolts' of the business on a day-to-day basis. In many businesses this requires a technical background but with a practical rather than a theoretical bias. In many businesses, also, the bulk of the manpower is employed in operations and so this branch often requires considerable man-management skill. Its prime role is to ensure that customers' orders are fulfilled economically and punctually.

Marketing management is concerned with selling the product or service – finding customers and persuading them to buy. It involves market research, advertising, selling and, sometimes, storage and distribution. Where a large sales force is employed, this also requires man-management skills. It needs to keep watch on and try to foresee activities of competitors. With a rapidly changing market, it is also closely involved in product or service development.

Finance management is concerned with raising funds and looking after them – paying creditors, collecting debts and paying wages and other expenses. In a young business, when money is scarce, this role is particularly important. Expenditure must be strictly controlled to provide money, not only for running the day-to-day business but also for expansion.

Personnel management is concerned with recruiting, training and developing staff and for discharging those not required or not up to standard. Its importance depends upon the size of the business and the industrial-relations climate in which the business runs. It must establish pay and conditions of employment which make the staff work loyally and effectively. One of its most important duties has become that of keeping abreast of and conforming to employment legislation. Like financial management, its role is often to devise policies and procedures which are carried out by others.

Administration management is concerned with the routine collection, storage and supply of information wherever it is needed within or even outside the business, e.g. government departments. It is frequently combined with financial management but this is by no means universal. In some businesses it is better centred in the operations or marketing functions. Increasingly it is becoming involved in personnel information. The use of computers can greatly assist this task in larger organizations but the introduction of unsuitable systems can complicate life needlessly in smaller businesses.

Obviously the mixture of management skills required will vary greatly from one business to another. Some skills may not be needed at all at the start of some businesses. You should think about the level of skill you personally can offer in each, since this will be a factor to consider when making a final choice of business.

I must emphasize here that I am talking of five branches of management – not five managers. In most small businesses, they will all be the responsibility of one person – the owner. In some cases, however, it may be wise to make someone else responsible for part of the load and in a partnership the duties will normally be shared among the partners.

Skills, knowledge and experience

In addition to the management expertise mentioned above,

each business has its own peculiar requirements of skills, knowledge and experience. There is a world of difference between the *amateur*, concerned with product quality but without much regard for how long it takes to produce or the materials used, and the *professional* who has to worry about rate of output and material costs. You must recognize the particular skills and knowledge required by the business you choose and take steps to fill any gaps in your experience.

Most businesses require other skills at times, e.g. advertising layout, coping with equipment breakdowns, property repair, vehicle maintenance. It is ideal if the entrepeneur can supply all of these himself but this is unlikely to happen in practice. Provided these are not in the main-stream running of the business, they can usually be provided on a part-time basis using friends, consultants or contractors.

CHAPTER 3

Finding Business Opportunities

Some readers may be keen to start a business and be well equipped to do so but have difficulty in finding the right idea. You don't have to choose something novel to be successful in starting a business. The late Sir Jack Cohen did nothing original when he started a grocery shop but he built it up into the highly successful Tesco Stores. But if you don't have to be original, you do have to be good at it – and you are more likely to be good at something you enjoy.

That is why I suggest you begin your search for a suitable business by looking at what interests you. This chapter gives a stepwise process which shows you how to (1) use your interests as a source of ideas, (2) convert the ideas into business propositions, (3) clarify what you want to get out of your business, (4) reduce the number of business propositions to a short list of favourites. Even if you already have one or more ideas in mind, it is worth going through these steps, since they may suggest new ideas or a new twist to an old idea.

Step 1: Brainstorming

Take a piece of paper and draw a line down the middle. Head the left half 'Interests' and the right half 'Business Ideas'. On the left-hand side write down all the leisure activities which interest you: hobbies (past or present), what you like reading about, what kind of TV programme you enjoy, how you like to spend your spare time, what you do on holiday, what sports you enjoy doing or watching . . . and so on.

Now sit back and look at what you have written down.

Think hard about each item in turn and in the right-hand column put down all the ideas you can think of which might be the subject of a business. For example, if cooking is one of your interests, this might suggest: home baking, catering, cookery demonstrating, restaurant.

During the brainstorming step, you should not attempt to criticize or censor your ideas. Write down everything that comes into your head, no matter how wild it may seem. There is no need to write a long description – just jot down a word or two to remind you of each idea.

The whole point is to keep the flow of inspiration going as long as possible. Keep the pot boiling. You can, if you wish, form this step into a game you play with family and friends. Often a group of people stimulate each other, an idea from one person triggering off another idea from someone else.

When the flow dries up, turn back to the left-hand column and write down all the jobs you have ever done which you enjoyed, including part-time and temporary work. Add any attractive jobs done by your family and friends. Think of the businesses run by various customers and suppliers you have encountered in your working career. Do any of them appeal to you?

Once again write down in the right-hand column all the different business ideas suggested by each interest. Continue until you run out of steam once more.

Repeat the zig-zag progression four times more, drawing your list of interests for the left-hand column in turn from: (1) subjects you have studied at school, college, evening classes or by correspondence course; (2) special activities in your district – industrial, commercial, agricultural or governmental; (3) any special skills or knowledge you possess, no matter how non-commercial they may seem at first sight; (4) your views on growth industries, technological change, new types of work.

Step 2: Converting ideas to propositions

You should now have a list of business ideas which may be long or short, depending upon the fertility of your imagination and the help you got from others. Some of them may seem pretty improbable but don't worry; many a good business has sprung from what seemed at first a crazy idea. The purpose of this step is to produce a number of reasonably practicable business propositions from your list of ideas.

You will probably find it helpful in this step to refer back to Chapter 2, in which the features of different types of business are discussed. These suggest various ways in which the same idea can be developed to produce a number of quite different business propositions.

This can best be illustrated by the example of Sally, who thought – and whose family agreed – that she made a rather tasty apple pie. She looked to see what business propositions she could develop, concerned with making, selling or providing some service connected with apple pies.

The nature of the product – apple pie – decreed that some of the features would be virtually constant for all propositions. It was not a novel product, it was perishable, it was relatively inexpensive (although there might be a premium for quality), it was in demand throughout the year, it was not subject to fashions and the ultimate consumer was the public (although it could be sold through several channels).

The features which seemed to offer most scope for variation were: *scale of business* (ranging from small batch to mass production); *product quality* (from inexpensive mass market to high-priced luxury models); *degree of standardization* (from a single model to a wide range of quality, size and type); *spread of market* (local, regional, national or even international); *brand* (could be trade marked or sold to 'own brand' buyers); *competition* (depending upon price and location); *innovation* (scope for devising new versions of a traditional dish).

After some head-scratching and conferring with others, Sally came up with the following list of possible business propositions:

MAKING PIES

   (1) make pies to order for customers' home freezers;

   (2) produce packaged frozen pies for freezer shops;

   (3) mass-produce individual pies for retail store and supermarket chains;

   (4) invent and produce an apple-pie mix;

SELLING PIES

   (5) sell home-baked pies in a roadside kiosk in summer;

   (6) sell home-baked pies from a weekly market stall;

   (7) open an 'Apple Pie Queen' shop with wide range of fresh pies daily;

   (8) start an 'Apple Pie Bar' chain for consumption of pie and coffee on or off the premises;

   (9) start a franchise operation for 'Apple Pie Bars';

PIE SERVICES

   (10) deliver individual pies daily to offices, factories, construction sites;

   (11) supply high-quality dessert pies to restaurants;

   (12) supply inexpensive dessert pies in bulk to factory canteens, schools, hospitals, etc.

Step 3: Clarifying objectives

You must now pause for a moment and think about what you want to get out of your new business. You want – and I want – your business to be a success, but what do *you* mean by success? Sometimes people put a great effort into creating a business which is successful in the sense that they make a great deal of money. Then they discover that this was not what they wanted at all. In achieving financial success, they have paid a high price in other ways – perhaps too high a price.

As mentioned in Chapter 1, a desire to make money is not the only reason why entrepreneurs start a business. The urge for independence is also a powerful motive, but independence to do what? In this step you should examine *your* motives and decide what *you* want to achieve. To put it in business jargon, you must decide on your objectives.

What kind of work do you want to do in your business? Do you want to work mainly with your hands or with your brain? Would you rather work outdoors or indoors? Do you want to work in the same place most of the time or do you want to travel around? Have you a particular skill or experience you enjoy using? Or are you equally willing to do any kind of work to ensure that your business flourishes?

You probably expect to have to work hard while the business is getting off the ground. But once it is running, are you prepared to continue working long hours, provided you get the financial reward, or is their a limit? Even during the initial period, must you restrict your hours because of family responsibilities, your own health or a preference for leisure? Are you reluctant, for any reason, to work in the evenings or at weekends?

If you intend to start a part-time business, how many hours a week can you work and how are these distributed? For instance, someone with a full-time job may only be available evenings and weekends, whereas a housewife may only be free during the hours her children are at school. Can you put in these hours all the year round or must they be cut at certain times, e.g. because of school holidays or seasonal overtime in your normal job?

Are you willing to sacrifice holidays for a year or two or

can you get someone else to run the business while you are on holiday? Alternatively, must you choose a business which can be closed for holidays?

Do you want to involve members of your family or do you prefer to keep business and family life apart? How much contact with other people do you seek in your business? Would you rather see the same people regularly or do you like meeting strangers – or are you a loner? Do you want to start a business which meets a real need in your community or don't you care as long as it is legal? Is it important to you what the neighbours think of your business?

I must make it clear that there are no 'good' and 'bad' answers to the above questions. All that matters is that you give answers which are honest and realistic for YOU. You should not feel guilty if you decide to start a business which gives you time off for your family or hobbies, provided you accept the fact that you will probably make less money and will have a narrower range of choice. As long as this is what you really want, you can be a success according to *your* objectives.

Step 4: Narrowing the field

During Step 1, you were urged not to apply any criticism to the stream of ideas, in case this caused the flow to dry up. It is time now to examine the business propositions developed in Step 2 and pick out the three or four which are most suitable for you. This criticism is based on what you have to offer (Chapter 1), what the businesses need (Chapter 2) and what you want to achieve (Step 3).

This process can best be illustrated by returning to the example of Sally and her twelve business propositions, all based on her skill at making apple pies. If you look again at these, you will see that each proposition differs from the others in certain respects. To find out which propositions were more suitable for her and which less suitable was Sally's next problem.

She decided that the ideal business for her would meet the following six objectives: (a) it would not require previous *business experience*; (b) it would not require previous *sales experience*; (c) it would need *little capital*; (d) it could be run on a *part-time* basis of not more than 5–6 hours a day; (e) it could be run on a 5-*day week*; (f) it would not interfere with family *holidays*, i.e. could be run by her sister or friends in her absence.

Sally then drew up a table (see Table I) and put against each proposition a cross for each objective which was met.

Table I – Screening Sally's business propositions

Propositions	Objectives						
	(a)	(b)	(c)	(d)	(e)	(f)	Score
(1) home freezers	x	x	x	x	x	x	6
(2) freezer shops				x	x	x	3
(3) supermarkets					x		1
(4) pie mix				x	x	x	3
(5) roadside kiosk	x	x	x			x	4
(6) market stall	x	x	x	x	x	x	6
(7) pie shop	x	x					2
(8) pie bar chain		x					1
(9) franchise							–
(10) offices	x		x	x	x	x	5
(11) restaurants	x	x	x	x		x	5
(12) canteens					x		1

You will see that two propositions met all six objectives, viz. (1) home freezers and (6) market stall. A further two propositions met five objectives and might, with a bit of ingenuity, be made fully acceptable. These were (10) offices and (11) restaurants. These four propositions formed Sally's short list for more detailed study along the lines described in Chapter 4.

What about franchising?

One way of solving the problem of thinking up a business proposition is to take up an idea which has already been shown to be successful. Some readers may therefore be attracted by the idea of franchising which, on the surface, offers to make the path of the entrepreneur that much smoother and to enhance the prospects of success. Indeed the British Franchise Association (BFA) claims that the small businessman has seven times the chance of success with a reputable franchise, compared with going it alone.

Franchising is based on the fact that an established business *concept* has a commercial value. This concept may be an idea, a trade name, a secret formula or process, or a piece of equipment. Examples of franchises in Britain are Wimpy, Holiday Inns, Dyno-Rod, Coca-Cola, Budget-Rent-a-Car, Kentucky Fried Chicken. The owner of this concept (the franchisor) makes an agreement with an entrepreneur (the franchisee) which permits the latter to start and run a business using the concept of the franchisor.

Ideally the franchise agreement has the following elements:

(a) Before concluding an agreement, the franchisor vets the applicant carefully, from a personal as well as a financial standpoint, to ensure that he has the qualities required to make a success of that particular business.

(b) The franchisee is given exclusive rights to use the franchisor's concept within a defined territory.

(c) For an initial fee, the franchisee gets all the help he needs to start the business, including: finding and fixing up suitable premises, raising finance, purchasing equipment and supplies, training for himself and staff, initial promotion.

(d) For an ongoing payment, the franchisor continues to

give help when required and provides certain central services, e.g. national or regional advertising. This payment is often linked to the turnover or profit of the business, giving the franchisor a vested interest in its growth.

(e) Ownership of the business is completely in the hands of the franchisee who must put up or borrow all the capital and to whom all the profit (after payment of the ongoing fee) accrues.

(f) The franchisor continues to exercise some control over the way the business is run, thus protecting its own long-term interests and those of other franchisees.

In this form, the appeal to the inexperienced would-be entrepreneur is obvious. In effect, he is buying instant know-how for an agreed fee, instead of 'picking it up' the hard way over a longer period at an unpredictable cost. Hopefully he can also avoid an initial period of, perhaps heavy, trading losses. The fact that he has passed the vetting process of the franchisor gives him confidence and he is given the business training he lacks. It is hardly surprising, therefore, that the demand for franchises is outstripping the supply.

Unfortunately, conditions are not always ideal. There has been a number of downright rackets, as the media have publicized extensively. Perhaps the worst have vanished, but it is arguable whether the terms of some of the franchises on offer really give the inexperienced entrepreneur a chance to make a fair return on the investment demanded, no matter how hard he works.

Nevertheless, franchises should not be ignored, since there are undoubtedly successes as well as failures. A good product or service, coupled with a fair franchise agreement, can give the budding entrepreneur a better start. What should be remembered is that the person who can benefit most from a franchise is handicapped by his inexperience when choosing and negotiating terms for a franchise. Before committing yourself, therefore, make sure you get a chance to have private discussions with existing franchisees and get agreements thoroughly vetted by your solicitor and accountant before signing anything.

CHAPTER 4

Picking the Winner

One sometimes sees businesses going bust or just limping along which, it seems obvious to the outsider, should never have been started. Yet few people start a business without thinking about it a great deal. The answer to this puzzle is sometimes bad luck but in most cases it is simply that the entrepreneur did not think about the right things.

The purpose of this chapter is to examine your short list of business propositions from several important aspects. This may cause you to discard some of them. A decision-making process is then described which will enable you to pick out which of the surviving propositions best fits your particular combination of abilities, interests and objectives.

Market demand

Someone recently opened a tropical fish shop in a small village near where I live. The owner was presumably interested in tropical fish and probably knew a lot about them. He may have been a good businessman in some respects but the surrounding countryside is not heavily populated nor is the local proportion of tropical fish fanciers, as far as I know, above the national average. The business closed in less than a year.

It is surprising how many would-be entrepreneurs fail to check on market demand before starting their business. The fact that you have the capital and the ability to run a particular business will not guarantee success if there are not enough customers who want your goods or service.

You cannot, of course, make a very accurate estimate of market demand but it is usually not difficult to make a rough

forecast which will show whether the business is at least possible. The secret is to spot how the market is related to
something you can easily find out, such as total population
(e.g. groceries), number of babies born (e.g. maternity wear),
number of new houses (e.g. landscape gardening), number
of households (e.g. DIY products), number of businesses
(e.g. office stationery).

First you decide upon your 'territory', i.e. the area within
which most of your customers will be located. You then find
out from local authority or government sources, the
numbers of population, houses or whatever you seek within
your territory. Finally you estimate the annual expenditure
per potential customer. In many cases this can be obtained
from the Family Expenditure Survey, issued by the Department of Employment and published annually by HMSO.

In other cases you may need to approach trade or hobby
magazine editors, trade associations, local chambers of trade
or other sources listed in Appendix 2. A little ingenuity may
be needed but it is surprising how much information can be
gathered from a few telephone calls.

It is of course unlikely that you will have no competitors.
Mark your 'territory' on a map and plot the position of each
competitor. How well entrenched are they and what is the
reputation of each? Estimate how the market is shared between your competitors at present. What share of the
market do you realistically think you could secure within,
say, a year?

Scale of business

The purpose of the above exercise is twofold. Firstly, it is to
check, as far as you can, that the potential market is big
enough to justify starting your business. Secondly, it is to
gain some idea of your *turnover*, i.e. how much money you
can expect to get from customers in a year.

There is also another way you can estimate turnover. For

instance, in many service businesses the price is based on the time taken, so you know how many pounds per hour you earn. Estimate how many hours per week you are earning, allowing for time spent on getting business, book-keeping, travelling, repairing equipment, etc. From this you can estimate your weekly turnover.

If you divide the annual turnover of a selling business by the average value of the goods in stock, you get the *stockturn rate*. This rate varies considerably, from about 1–2 in the antique trade to perhaps 20–30 in food supermarkets. For each type of business, there is a typical rate which can be used to estimate the amount of stock needed to achieve a given turnover. For example, for a stockturn rate of 2.5 and a turnover of £50,000,

$$\text{average stock} = \frac{\text{turnover}}{\text{stockturn rate}} = \frac{£50,000}{2.5} = £20,000$$

The difference between the buying and selling price of an article, expressed as a percentage of the selling price, is known as the *profit margin*. This also varies widely from one type of business to another and one finds, for instance, that goods with a low stockturn rate (e.g. furniture) have a high margin. Other factors also come into play, such as risk of goods going out of fashion (e.g. teenage clothes) or stock spoilage (e.g. greengroceries) . . . or competition!

Using a typical profit margin for your particular business, you can estimate roughly the *gross trading profit* one can expect from a given turnover. For example, for an annual turnover of £50,000 and a profit margin of 25 per cent,

$$\begin{aligned}
\text{gross trading profit} &= \text{profit margin} \times \text{turnover} \\
&= 25 \text{ per cent} \times £50,000 \\
&= £12,500 \text{ per annum}
\end{aligned}$$

Capital requirements

Having decided the scale of your business, you can now estimate your capital requirements. First, the *fixed capital*.

From the turnover, you can estimate the floorspace you need for equipment, for storage and for working purposes. Can you rent this? If not, how much will it cost to buy and what proportion can be covered by a mortgage? What will it cost to fix up your premises? What production or selling capacity should you install and what does this mean in terms of machinery, tools, fittings, transport, office equipment, etc.

You will also need *working capital* to pay for initial stocks of raw materials or goods for sale, which you can estimate as described above. From the turnover and profit margin you can estimate the rate at which money is flowing out to pay wages and buy new stocks and flowing in from customers. The usual practices in the trade will indicate how long a time lag to expect, from which you can calculate the working capital needed to bridge the gap.

How does the total of fixed plus working capital compare with what you can provide? Are your funds adequate or is there a shortfall which must be supplied by the means described in Chapter 6?

Income and expenditure

Before studying the business income and expenditure, you should first draw up a domestic budget for the next twelve months. Rule up a large sheet of paper into fourteen vertical columns: one for the list of items, one for each month and one for the annual total. Under the heading 'Expenditure', list everything you can think of under each month, jogging your memory with bank statements, cheque stubs, receipts, etc.

One must compromise between the desire for a detailed picture and the avoidance of an excessive number of small items – usually about twelve to fifteen items are sufficient. If this is the first time you have made a budget, better insert an 'unforeseen' item for 5 or 10 per cent of the total. This budget is intended to show the situation after you have started your business, so adjust such entries as travelling expenses and canteen meals.

Under the heading 'Income', list the amount under the expected month of receipt for those sources which you expect to continue after starting your business – salary of spouse, building society interest, investments, etc. To keep it simple, these should be entered after deduction of tax. Subtracting 'Income' from 'Expenditure' will show you what contribution the business must make to domestic expenses or vice versa.

You should now work out on a fresh sheet of paper an annual budget for the business, based on your target turnover. Under 'Expenditure', list all the items associated with running the business, such as: wages and related costs (NHI contributions, luncheon vouchers, expenses, overtime and bonus payments, etc.); operating supplies, raw materials or components and goods for sale; rent, rates and insurance; heating and lighting; telephone, postage, stationery and sundries; advertising and promotion; repairs and spare parts; transport and hire of equipment; bank charges, loan interest and HP payments.

Under 'Income', list your turnover (less any sales commission) plus any other sources of business income expected. To keep this simple, it is better to deduct VAT from both income and expenditure items affected by VAT. If you do not expect to register for VAT, then you should not deduct it from expenditures since you cannot recover it.

Deducting expenditure from income gives your *gross profit*. From this you have to deduct *depreciation* or, as the tax inspector now calls it, *capital allowances*. This gives you the *net taxable profit*. How does this compare with the amount needed to balance the domestic budget? How does it compare with your present salary before tax? What is the *return on investment* before tax, i.e. net taxable profit expressed as a percentage of your capital investment? (By way of a yardstick, building societies have been paying over 10 per cent before tax for most of the past five years – and giving high security.)

The decision-making process

The survivors from your short list have passed the test of market demand, capital requirements and profitability. To select the best one of these, you may be able to apply the method used by Sally in Chapter 3. More likely, you feel the need for a better method. How can one compare, say, a welding business, a typing bureau, running a toyshop, TV servicing or whatever? Surely that is just like comparing apples and pears?

When you think about it, however, it is not so difficult to compare apples and pears. In fact, millions of housewives do this every day. They compare them on the basis of price, freshness and the tastes of their families. So you see, apples and pears can be compared if you use the right *criteria*, i.e. the measures used for comparison.

The choice of these, and the relative importance you attach to each, is a very personal thing. The following list of commonly used criteria is therefore given merely as an illustration:

> capital investment required; anticipated net profit; security of income; opportunity for growth; work satisfaction; use of existing skills; chance to learn new skills; variety of work; contact with other people; where you will work; where you will live; amount of leisure time; length of holidays; flexibility of working hours; possibility of working part-time; outdoor work; effect on health; opportunity for travel; provision of employment for family; possibility of accumulating capital.

Having selected the criteria which seem most important to you, consider each in turn. Are any of them absolutely essential? For instance, you may feel that you cannot afford to consider any scheme which does not offer the prospect of earning at least £5,000 per annum – or £10,000 – or whatever your figure is. Perhaps lack of capital rules out any project needing more than x thousand – or hundred – pounds. Or family responsibilities may dictate that only part-time businesses can be considered.

Most people will have only two or three *essential criteria*, but you can select any number you like, provided that they really are ones on which you cannot or will not give way. Compare each of your propositions in turn against these essential criteria and scrap any which fails to meet them.

The next step is to draw up a list of *desirable criteria*. Sometimes your essential criteria should now be ignored, e.g. once a business meets a part-time requirement, you may no longer be interested in this criterion. Sometimes they should remain, e.g. although a scheme has met the minimum net profit test, you may still be interested in how much the profit is likely to be.

List your desirable criteria in order of importance, starting with the most important. The ideal number is between six and ten. Fewer than six does not give sufficient discrimination. More than ten adds to the work and, since the extra ones are the least important, they are unlikely to influence your decision. So if your list has less than six criteria, think again if you have overlooked any. If there are more than ten cross off the bottom ones.

You are not likely to regard all these criteria as equally important. To allow for this it is necessary to introduce what are called *weighting factors*. Put '5' against the criterion at the top of your list – the most important one. Put '1' against the bottom criterion – the least important one. Put a number in the range of '1' to '5' against each of the other criteria. The second one need not be '4'; it could be '5' if this is very nearly equal to the first item in importance. It could be '3' if it is much less important than the first item.

The next step in the process is best shown by an example. Take the case of George, an experienced car mechanic working in a small garage whose present owner was retiring. This had unsettled George, who thought this might be the time to use the bit of capital he had scraped together to start his own business. He had narrowed down his choice to three schemes, all connected with cars since this was his greatest interest.

CASE A – REPAIR GARAGE
His present employer had offered George the chance of buying the business by putting £5,000 down and paying the balance of £15,000 over the next five years.

CASE B – CAR ACCESSORY SHOP
Open a shop selling car accessories and spare parts for the DIY motorist. To fit a shop and stock it would cost £6,000.

CASE C – HOME TUNING SERVICE
Run a mobile service, tuning customers' cars in their own garages. To buy a van and all the equipment would cost £4,000.

George had also been offered a job in the maintenance shop of a local transport contractor. Since he was not quite sure whether he really should start his own business, he put this into the comparison as *Case D – Maintenance job* to see how it would turn out.

He had only one essential criterion, viz. that the schemes should not require more capital than he had available. All the propositions met this criterion.

Somewhat naturally, George's interests and prejudices influenced his selection of desirable criteria and the weighting factors assigned to them. He was aged thirty-five and not greatly concerned about security; he felt that, as a skilled craftsman, he could easily get a job. In any case, his wife had a part-time job which ensured some cash flow into the house. He had a passion for fishing and hoped for more time to indulge it; he did not mind evening or weekend work to make up for this. He enjoyed working with his hands but disliked paperwork.

Against this background, he chose as follows:

criteria	*weighting factor*
interesting work	5
freedom from paperwork	4
variety of work	3
flexible working hours	3
contact with new people	2
anticipated income	2
security of income	1

George then drew up a decision table (Table II). For each of the four cases he studied there are two columns, one headed 'Points' and one headed 'Score'. The figures in the table have been obtained in the following way.

(a) For the first criterion, decide which of the four cases best meets that criterion. In this example the criterion 'work interest' is best met by Case C.

(b) Put 5 in the Points column under Case C.

(c) Decide how many points to give Cases A, B and D if C rates 5. In the example, A is rated at 4, B at 3 and D at 2.

(d) Repeat the process for each criterion in turn.

(e) Taking Case A, multiply the number of points for the first criterion by the weighting factor for that criterion $(4 \times 5 = 20)$ and put the answer in the Score column.

(f) Repeat for each criterion in turn under Case A.

(g) Total the score for Case A.

(h) Repeat the process for Cases B, C and D.

In George's case, this method ranks the four cases in the following order:

1st   Case C – Tuning service;

2nd   Case A – Repair garage;
3rd   Case B – Accessories shop;
4th   Case D – Maintenance job.

Incidentally, the decision table shows how much the outcome depends upon the criteria chosen and the weightings attached to them. For instance, someone with strong ambition, willing to work long hours and to accept the burden of paperwork, would almost certainly find Case A the most attractive. Alternatively, the person seeking a sheltered indoor job with steady hours would probably opt for Case B.

Table II.   George's decision table

Desirable Criteria	Weighting Factor	Case A Repair Garage		Case B Accessory Shop		Case C Tuning Service		Case D Maintenance Job	
		Points	Score	Points	Score	Points	Score	Points	Score
work interest	5	4	20	3	15	5	25	2	10
no paperwork	4	1	4	3	12	5	20	5	20
work variety	3	5	15	2	6	4	12	1	3
flexible hours	3	3	9	0	0	5	15	0	0
new people	2	5	10	5	10	5	10	3	6
income	2	5	10	2	4	3	6	1	2
security	1	4	4	3	3	2	2	5	5
Total score			72		50		90		46

Review of results

When you have done the exercise with *your* business propositions, look hard at the ranking that comes out. Are you happy to accept this answer? If not, why not? Go back over the working to make sure there is no mistake in the calculations. Look again at the criteria you have chosen. Is there some other important criterion that you have overlooked? Have you any second thoughts about the weighting factors you adopted?

Before deciding to start a particular business, there is one final step – examine the risks involved. Try to think of all the serious things which might go wrong and then assess each risk on (a) *probability* (how likely is it to happen?) and (b) *consequences* (if it does happen, how serious will it be?). Sometimes this may cause you to discard the favourite shown by the decision table (because there is a high probability of a serious risk occurring) and select a safer second string.

It may transpire that two of the schemes come out 'top equal' or nearly so. In this case, go back over the calculations, the criteria and the weighting factors to see if you have made any mistakes or if you want to change your mind. If this does not produce a clear favourite, then look at the risks to see if one is much safer. If you still find it hard to decide then toss for it!

Part II: Starting Your Business

CHAPTER 5
A Matter of Form

Before you start in business, you must decide what form your business will take. Three forms are legally possible: *sole trader, partnership, limited company.* In most new businesses you have a choice, so you must decide which form seems most suitable for you. The original decision is not irrevocable and you can change the form later. In fact, you may deliberately decide to start the business, say, as a partnership with the intention of changing it into a limited company at a later date.

If you are careless or ignorant, however, and choose a form which is unsuitable at the start, it will cost you time and money to put it right. The growth of your enterprise could even be set back. Therefore it is worth a bit of thinking and discussion with your accountant and solicitor at the outset.

The purpose of this chapter is to help you with this thinking, to explain the differences between the three forms, discuss the advantages and disadvantages of each and suggest some points you might consider before making your decision.

Sole trader

This does not mean, as the name suggests, that you are a one-man-band. You can have as many people working for you as you like – and as your business needs. Some sole traders run a very large business indeed.

What it does mean is that the owner is solely responsible for the business and for the actions of employees in carrying out the business. He is liable for its debts and the profits are taxed as his personal income.

On the other hand, he is undoubtedly the boss. He is not obliged to consult anyone else about how he runs it. If he does consult anyone – and it is often wise to do so – the final decision is still his responsibility.

Setting up such a business can be very simple. You just start keeping accounting records, which need not be elaborate. You are not obliged to have an auditor to check your accounts, although you will probably find it helpful to do so. It is usually wise to open a business bank account, separate from your personal account, although this is not obligatory. You should notify the Inspector of Taxes when you start a new business, either as sole trader or in partnership – get a copy of pamphlet IR28.

Partnership

There are various reasons why you may decide to start your business as a partnership. You may not feel sufficiently confident to go it alone but be happy to start the venture with a friend to share the responsibility. One of you may supply the special knowledge on which the business is based while the other supplies the capital. In its extreme form, the latter may take no active part in running the business and be what is called a 'sleeping partner'.

Some of the most successful partnerships are where the partners complement each other in experience or temperament. For instance one may be very skilled with his hands and looks after the manufacturing side of the business while the other is good in dealing with other people and looks after the sales. Or one may be very imaginative, producing one bright idea a minute, while the other is down-to-earth and selects which ideas to follow and which to reject.

But, just as in marriage, not all business partnerships are

successful. Such failures are not only caused by poor business – they can fail for personal reasons. A difference in temperament which is helpful to the business may make it difficult for partners to get along with each other on a personal plane.

An overworked active partner may grow to resent the sleeping partner who does nothing – but takes a share of the profits. A busy manufacturer may not understand why the sales partner spends so much time and money – *their* money – in entertaining customers. The creative partner may begin to hate the dull plodder who shoots down all his best ideas.

So you must choose your partner with care – preferably someone you have known well for a long time. Any act by one partner on behalf of the business – a promise made, a debt incurred, money paid – is binding on the other partners. You must trust your partner and feel comfortable in doing so. For these reasons, partners are usually chosen from among the family, close friends or business associates.

Whenever two or more people go into business together, a partnership is created. Forming a partnership is simple and cheap but getting out of a partnership is much more complicated and expensive. Although there is no legal obligation, therefore, it is common to get a solicitor to draw up a *Partnership Agreement*. A well-formulated (which need not mean complicated) agreement can remove most of the common sources of friction within a partnership.

For instance, the partners can record how they wish to deal with such matters as division of profits, payment of salaries, interest on capital, etc. In the absence of such an agreement, express or implied, the provisions of the Partnership Act 1890 apply. This latter stipulates that partners are entitled to share equally in the capital and in the profits of the business.

It is not uncommon for partners to put in different amounts of capital, to devote different amounts of time or to carry different degrees of responsibility. These different contributions to the business are usually recognized by distributing the profits according to an agreed formula. This might stipulate, for example, what rate of interest should be paid on the capital contribution of each partner, what salary should be paid to each active partner and what should be done with any profits in excess of these sums. It might also lay down what to do in the event of a dispute between partners.

There is also a special type of *limited partnership*, in which a limited partner is liable for the partnership debts only to the amount of capital he has contributed. (If he withdraws any part of his capital during the partnership, however, he is liable to account for the amount so withdrawn.) A limited partner is not entitled to take part in the management of a partnership and if he does so, he will become liable as a general partner. He may, however, give advice regarding the conduct of the business.

Limited company

The main point which distinguishes a limited company from the other two forms is that it is regarded as a *separate legal entity* from the people who own and run it. It is treated as if it were a separate person which, as you will see below, has certain implications. There are two kinds of companies – public companies and private companies.

Public companies are those whose shares can be bought and sold by the public, usually through the Stock Exchange, such as ICI or Marks & Spencer. As a consequence of the 1980 Companies Act, the name of a public company must end with the words 'public limited company' or 'PLC'. (Don't be misled, however, by the fact that some public companies have not yet completed the changeover of their signs, stationery, etc. from Ltd to PLC.)

Companies whose shares are not on sale to the public are called *private companies*. Two or more persons may form a private company with limited liability by subscribing their names to a Memorandum of Association, taking at least one share each in the company and registering the company in accordance with the Acts. This latter is the form you may consider for setting up your business.

You must put the word 'Limited' at the end of the company name. This shows everyone that it is a *limited liability company*, i.e. the liability of a shareholder is limited to the amount of his or her shareholding. It is only fair to warn you, however, that banks often ask for a personal guarantee to cover any loans made to a newly formed company, which may defeat the object of the exercise.

There are certain formalities you must observe when forming a company. You must have a *Memorandum of Association* which sets out the objects of the company, i.e. the kind of business you intend to run. While you should have a clear idea of the limitations of the business at the outset, you do not want to be so restricted that you cannot take advantage of unforeseen opportunities which may arise in future, since you are not legally permitted to carry on any activity not covered by the Memorandum. Consequently you should draft this sufficiently widely to embrace anything you might remotely want to do.

You must have *Articles of Association* which govern the internal running of the company, i.e. the procedures for holding meetings, voting, issuing shares, transferring shares, auditing accounts, altering the nominal capital, etc. Standard regulations have been drawn up in Companies Acts and most companies follow one of these standards, although it is sometimes necessary to modify these to meet your needs.

Other documents needed with your application include *Statement of Capital, Statement of First Directors and Secretary and intended situation of Registered Office* and *Declaration of Compliance*.

Once you have complied with the requirements and paid the appropriate fees you may obtain a *Certificate of Incorporation*, which is issued by the Registrar of Companies, Companies House, Crown Way, Maindy,

Cardiff CF4 3UZ. For Companies whose registered office is in Scotland, applications should be addressed to the Registrar of Companies, Exchequer Chambers, George Street, Edinburgh EH2 3DJ. Until this certificate is issued, the company does not legally exist. Apart from complying with the various regulations of the Companies Acts, issue depends a lot upon the choice of a suitable name for your company. To be acceptable, this must not be inappropriate for the objects of the company, nor may you use the name of an existing or defunct company or one very like it.

All of the above sounds pretty intimidating but it is not as bad as it seems. If you want to form a small, fairly straightforward company the simplest and probably the cheapest way to do so is to use a *company registration agent* (look up the Yellow Pages). When you tell him the kind of business you want to run, he will pick out from his files a suitable draft Memorandum and submit it to you for approval. Once this is agreed, he will carry out the formalities and present you with all the finished documents as a complete package.

You are strongly advised to discuss this draft Memorandum with your solicitor or accountant before agreeing to it, because any errors or omissions can be costly. Indeed the whole field of company law is becoming so complicated that it may be wiser to employ, through your solicitor or accountant, the services of a firm which specializes in company formation. Such professional advice by specialists, particularly if your needs are in any way out of the ordinary, will ensure a company tailored to your particular requirements.

Advantages and disadvantages

Having described the three legal forms your business may take, let us now look at the advantages and disadvantages of each.

SOLE TRADER

The obvious advantage is that there is only one boss – YOU. Once you have decided something, you do not have to persuade partners or co-directors to agree. It is easy to present a clear and convincing business image, based on your own personality and philosophy. It is cheap and easy to start your business and, in most cases, a simple form of book-keeping is adequate.

If you start up in the middle of the tax year, you may offset your starting losses against previous earnings in that tax year. If you use part of your home for business purposes, the tax inspector will probably agree that a proportionate share of the domestic running costs can be charged to the business.

On the other hand you, as the sole boss, must carry the sole responsibility. There is no one else to share the problems. Nor is there anyone in the business with sufficient weight to stimulate you when your efforts flag or to stop you from acting unwisely. If you are sick or want to have a holiday, your income may stop altogether or, at best, may depend upon the efforts of an employee with far less at stake than you.

If you are successful and your profits soar, they may be subject to the highest rates of personal taxation. And any money you plough back into the business must come from what is left after tax. If you go bust, your business creditors can claim on your personal possessions – house, furniture, clothes, etc.

PARTNERSHIP

A partnership has the advantage of greater resources than a sole trader in terms of man-hours, knowledge, experience and probably money. Where the partners complement each other's strengths and weaknesses, as they should, a good partnership can offer a wider range of skills than most sole traders.

Partners can cover for each other when sick or on holiday, so that the earnings continue throughout the year. The need to persuade partners in advance – or at least to justify your actions afterwards – tends to result in better decisions, even if they are sometimes made more slowly. Partnerships also provide an opportunity to share worries and discuss problems with someone who is equally knowledgeable and concerned.

Partnerships are particularly common in some professions and some firms have been in existence for a long time. As older partners retire, they are replaced by younger ones, resulting in an age progression through the partnership. Thus younger partners may join at a cost they can afford and retired partners may continue to draw an income from the partnership.

The main disadvantage of a partnership is that it is very hard to find the right partners. Partners must be sufficiently different in skills and temperament to be able to complement one another but not so different as to be unable to work together in harness.

Just like the sole trader, each partner has unlimited financial liability for the business. If the business goes bust, the creditors can claim on the personal possessions of each and every partner, regardless of who is to blame for the failure. Even if one partner only is entirely at fault – and admits it – the personal possessions of all are in jeopardy. With that hanging over you, you must have partners you can trust because if you can't trust them you are going to feel very worried.

If the partners are out of step with each other, the business is harder to run efficiently. In a divided family, children may try to play one parent off against the other. In a disunited partnership, one may find customers, suppliers and employees all trying to exploit their differences.

LIMITED COMPANY

The main advantage of a company is its separate legal existence. If the business folds up, you are unlikely to have your house and other personal possessions seized to pay creditors. If it is successful, some of the profits can be retained in the business without being exposed to the highest personal rates of tax. Losses in bad years can be carried forward and offset against profits in good years. If anything should happen to you – or you wish to retire – the company can continue the business as long as someone can be found to run it.

In the eyes of many people, a company seems more substantial than a one-man business and this may influence suppliers and customers in your favour. It is possible to attract more capital by selling some of your shares or creating new ones, without your losing control of the business.

On the other hand, to meet the requirements of the Companies Act means keeping more complicated accounts than those of a sole trader. It also takes time and money, which cannot be charged to the company itself, to set up a company. Moreover, on payment of a small fee anyone – customer, supplier or competitior – can obtain from Companies House details of your past profits, nominal capital and names of shareholders and directors.

Which form is best for you?

This is a key question, the answer to which can affect the future success of your business. What factors should you consider before making up your mind? The first is the nature of the business itself. Certain professional bodies prohibit their members (e.g. accountants, solicitors) from operating as limited companies – they must accept unlimited liability for the service they offer: in such cases, the choice is between sole trader and partnership. Outside the professional sphere, few such restrictions exist.

The number of people involved in starting the business is obviously important. If Tom, Dick and Harry are all giving up secure jobs to embark together on a new business, Dick and Harry are unlikely to agree that Tom should be the sole owner while they become salaried employees. If Dick and Harry are putting in some capital it becomes virtually certain that they will want to be partners or directors.

Another factor is the scale of operation. If you are starting off with one or two people only, possibly even on a part-time basis, you want to spend as much time as possible on productive work. This means keeping your book-keeping as simple as you dare. Why saddle yourself with the extra paperwork demanded by a partnership or limited company?

Your personal tax position should also be considered. Many businesses make a loss during the early days, no matter how successful they may be later. Under a recent revision to the tax rules, these losses can be offset against tax paid under PAYE during the three years before starting your business. This applies only to those starting as sole traders or partnerships, not to a limited company, since you and the company are, in law, different people.

The amount of capital required – and the method of raising it – can have a decisive influence. If a modest sum is needed, which you can raise on a personal basis, you have a free choice as to form. If you need additional capital from another person who wishes to be associated with the business, whether in an active or 'sleeping' capacity, then you must form a partnership or limited company. If your venture is on such a scale that you are being assisted by a merchant bank or similar agency, they may well insist upon your forming a limited company in which they can hold shares.

All of the above factors may, to a greater or lesser extent, play a role in your final choice of form. The most important factor in all cases, however, is your own temperament. If you have carried out the exercises in Chapter 1, you should have a reasonably good assessment of yourself. This assessment should be used in making your final decision.

The fact that you are considering starting your own business shows that you have some desire for independence.

How strong is your desire? Some entrepreneurs are almost fanatical, which is both a strength and a weakness. This urge provides the drive which keeps them going, working very long hours and refusing to be beaten by the series of adverse blows which occur so exasperatingly during the first few years of most businesses.

It is also the weakness which blinds them to difficulties which are foreseen by others and deafens them to advice from anyone else, however well-meaning. If you have tendencies in this direction, you had better become a sole trader or set up a limited company in which you hold the control.

On the other hand, you may be the kind of person who likes to share both troubles and successes. Perhaps you recognize your limitations and seek to combine with someone else of different make-up and experience to produce a team which is stronger than the individual members. You may feel happier in the knowledge that, should you fall sick or go on holiday, you can leave the business in the hands of someone as committed to the enterprise as you are. Provided you know the right partner and can trust each other, you will rightly prefer to set up a partnership or a limited company with an equitable share of the capital and reponsibilities.

What will you call your business?

Whatever form you choose for your business, you must decide what to call it. A rose may smell as sweet by any other name but this is not true in the business world. Marks & Spencer is now a highly respected name in its field but it took the company a long time to achieve this. The much more rapid rise of Mothercare owes at least something to the clever choice of name.

If your name is John Smith, you can start your business under the name of John Smith without formality. If Smith, Jones and Robinson wish to go into partnership under the name of Smith, Jones and Robinson, they may do so forthwith. But if a sole trader, partnership or company wishes to trade under a name other than their own surname(s) or full corporate name, certain formalities must be observed.

Regulations which came into force on 26 February 1982 require that in such cases the correct name of the business owner must be disclosed, whether the owner be sole trader, partnership or company. In addition, a business or other address must be given at which documents may be served if necessary. This information must be shown in legible characters on all business letters, written orders, invoices, receipts and written demands for payments.

The information must also be displayed prominently at any premises where the business is carried on and to which customers and suppliers have access. If anyone with whom the business has dealings asks for the name and address of the owner, these must be supplied immediately in writing. These formalities are not difficult to carry out. It is simply a matter of remembering to do them but it is important because there are penalties for failing to do so.

There is one point which sometimes causes confusion. As a sole trader, you may call yourself 'John Smith and Company'. This must be treated as a business name but you would still be a sole trader – not a limited company. Similarly with a partnership. It is the word 'Limited' which is compulsory in the names of all limited companies – not the word 'Company'.

Of course your own name may be so well known in your own line of business that you would be foolish to use any other. This is, however, the exception. In most cases the choice of a catchy and easily remembered name can help your business to grow, so it is worth a bit of thought.

CHAPTER 6

Where to Get the Money

There is a great argument about whether or not there is sufficient money available for starting new businesses and whether budding entrepreneurs encounter excessive difficulty in getting what they need. One does hear of people who experience great difficulty in raising finance for new ventures. On the other hand, I know of entrepreneurs being able to get all the financial support they need, sometimes with surprising ease. Personally, I think that if you have a sound proposition it is worth having a good try at raising the money. This chapter aims to help you do just that.

The likelihood of your being able to get the finance you need depends upon how much you need, what you want it for, your choice of source and how well you present your case. (It also depends upon how well you appear to have handled money in the past in previous business ventures or in your personal bank account.) The calculations you did in Chapter 4 tell you how much you need and what you want it for. The significance of the latter is that it affects the security you can offer. It also tells the lender how easily he could recover his money should you fall flat on your face, which obviously affects his willingness to lend.

Your own true worth

The first source of capital is yourself. So take a sheet of paper and list what you are worth. I do not suggest you sink your all in the venture but, for reasons which will become apparent, you ought to know what your total resources are.

To stimulate your thinking, write down the following headings and any others which occur to you. Put against each one your estimate of their current market value, less any selling expenses. Remember to deduct any HP or credit payments outstanding.

> cash in hand, bank current and deposit accounts, building society accounts, national and trustee savings bank accounts, savings certificates, premium bonds, unit trusts, stocks and shares, life insurance policies, pension contributions, house (less outstanding mortgage), car, furniture and furnishings, domestic equipment, clothes, sports and hobby equipment, jewellery, collections of stamps, coins, etc.

If you are married, some of these may be owned jointly with your spouse. Discuss the matter and, if your spouse is wholly behind your project, draw up three lists – 'his', 'hers' and 'joint'. If your spouse does not want to put his or her resources behind you, then you should make two lists, one for your own resources and one for your share of joint resources.

Having found out how much you are worth, the next step is to decide how much of the resources you want to commit to your enterprise. Split your total into three parts: (a) the sum you will make available for the business as soon as it can usefully be used; (b) the sum you are willing, however reluctantly, to use if necessary; (c) the sum you want to preserve for other purposes (e.g. children's education, somewhere to live) in the event of business collapse.

The first part should be held in an easily realizable form, e.g. bank or building society accounts. The second part may be less easily realizable but still in a form which can be used as security for a loan or guarantee. The third part must be put in a form where it cannot be touched in the event of business failure, such as a trust fund or in the name of your spouse (provided the latter is not involved in the ownership of the business).

Other sources of capital

If the first part of your own resources is not sufficient to meet the total capital requirement, you must find money from elsewhere. The first person to whom most entrepreneurs turn is their bank manager. Broadly speaking, the High Street banks lend money in two ways – overdrafts and term loans.

An *overdraft* arrangement gives you permission to overdraw your account at any time up to an agreed limit without further permission being needed. You pay interest only on the amount which is outstanding – not the agreed total – and the rate will fluctuate in step with the bank's current lending rate. For a relatively small new business you will probably have to pay 4 per cent more than the base lending rate. You may have to pay an initial fee and/or an annual fee while the arrangement is in force. Owing to the flexibility inherent in an overdraft, this method of borrowing is particularly well suited to *working capital* requirements.

With a *term loan*, the bank lends you a fixed sum for a fixed period, usually at a fixed rate of interest. You may arrange to repay the loan in steps during its lifetime or as a lump sum at the end. You must take the whole loan at the outset, whether you use it or not, but you cannot be obliged to repay it before the end of the term. A term loan is therefore appropriate for purchasing something (e.g. lease, piece of equipment) which will last at least as long as the loan and where you need the full loan at the beginning. Term loans are therefore well suited to *fixed capital* investment.

Although the clearing banks are the most common source of funds for small businesses, there are many other sources which may be used instead of, or in addition to, bank facilities. Many people occupy houses bought at a price well below today's market value. By *remortgaging your house* you can obtain an advance related to present-day values which, after repayment of the old mortgage, leaves you with a cash sum which you can use as you wish. This will of course increase your mortgage payments but building society interest rates are almost always lower than bank lending rates.

If you have a *life insurance* or *endowment policy* which has been in force for some years, there are various ways in which this can provide some cash. You may deposit the policy as security with a bank or building society to obtain a bigger loan than you would otherwise get.

You may borrow from the insurance company itself, often on more attractive terms than those offered by other lenders. Usually such loans need not be repaid until the policy matures. In both of the above cases, the policy remains in force, you continue the premium payments and, on maturity, you get the final payment less any loan which is still outstanding.

Alternatively, you can surrender the policy. The insurance company pays you the surrender value, you cease to pay premiums and the policy is no longer valid. The surrender terms are, however, often unattractive and it is usually better to borrow than surrender, provided you can keep up the premium payments.

If your policy is a large one, you may be able to sell it. Although little published, auctions of life insurance policies are held periodically. Auction prices are usually better than surrender values but you must of course give up all the benefits. The buyer keeps up the premiums and eventually collects the final payment.

In addition to the London and Scottish clearing banks, there is a large range of organizations which provide capital in different ways. *Short-term loans* and *overdraft facilities* are offered by a number of *investment banks*. Because of their short-term nature, such forms of finance are not usually recommended in starting a business, although they might be useful in overcoming a temporary problem.

Interest rates may be higher than those charged by the clearing banks.

Term loans over five to ten years are offered by many *merchant banks* and *investment banks*. A good credit rating is usually demanded and, since by definition new businesses have no track record, these sources are probably only available to the entrepreneur who has a personal track record.

Mortgage loans for businesses are obtainable from *insurance companies* and *investment companies*. They are usually repayable over a specified period, either by direct payments or by an insurance policy. If the latter, there may be a condition that all insurance business is done with the lender. If the value of the property does not provide enough security, you may have to show evidence that you will make enough profit to 'service' the loan, i.e. to be able to pay the interest and repay the capital.

Some lenders are willing to provide finance in the form of *equity capital*, i.e. they buy shares in the company. When it is a new company, this is usually called *venture capital* and there are investment companies who specialize in this. This may be attractive to the borrower since interest need only be paid, in the form of dividends, once profits are being made. It may be attractive to the lender, since if the company is successful the shares may become worth much more than was paid for them.

The cost of investigating a client's credit-worthiness and evaluating a business proposition is not proportional to the size of the business. Consequently, many lenders set a minimum figure on the loans they are prepared to handle, which puts them above the range of many new businesses. There are, however, three concerns which are willing to handle quite small loans – the Council for Small Industries in Rural Areas (CoSIRA) (see Appendix 2), ICFC (a division of Investors in Industry PLC) and its technical sister Venture Division.

Reducing capital needs

Inability to raise enough capital – or the unattractive terms on which it is offered – may cause you to have second thoughts. Is there no way in which you can reduce your need for capital to match what you can get? There is indeed; in fact there are several ways. Study each of the following suggestions in turn to see if it is feasible in your business and, if so, what the consequences would be – in both financial and non-financial terms.

(a) CUT OUT FAT
Go through your plans and estimates ruthlessly to find the 'fat' which can be cut out. Are you too perfectionist? Are you buying for appearance instead of need? Can you buy cheaper equipment or material which is good enough? Can you buy second-hand equipment? Do you really need to buy that spare – can you hire one as, when and if you need it? Can you learn to haggle a bit harder over prices? (This is an exercise you will have to do many times in future – better learn to do it properly now!)

(b) SCALE OF BUSINESS
Assess what turnover would correspond to the capital you can get. Repeat your estimated profit and cash-flow calculations. Is it feasible?

(c) OUTLAY ON PREMISES
Can you rent premises instead of buying? If you already own the premises, can you arrange a 'sale and lease-back' deal, i.e. someone buys the premises and rents it to you on agreed terms? Can you sub-let part of the premises? Can you find somewhere to work that is smaller or crummier – but cheaper? Are your fittings too luxurious? Can you dream up a new decor which looks as good but costs less? Can you do more of the fitting and decorating yourself?

(d) LEASING EQUIPMENT

Can you lease equipment instead of buying? If you must buy, can you do it on HP? Can you rent equipment you use only occasionally? Can you contract out some jobs to save buying the equipment? Can any equipment be shared with someone else?

(e) COST OF STOCKS

Have you really got the best credit terms from your supplier? Have you tried to see what others will offer? Can you get supplies 'on consignment', i.e. you don't pay for them until you sell them? Can you carry smaller stocks, backed up by a rapid delivery/collection service? Can you modify your stock control system to permit running with lower stocks?

(f) SALES POLICY

Think again about the sales policy you propose to adopt. Can you narrow the range of models you offer to reduce stocks? Can you concentrate on cash sales or cash with order, instead of credit sales? Can you offer a generous discount for prompt payment (see Chapter 20)? Can you choose a different class of market which will pay more promptly?

(g) COMMERCIAL DISCOUNT SERVICES

There is a variety of commercial services, by means of which you can receive prompt payment on invoices or bills, leaving someone else to chase up your debtors. These services include: acceptance credits, bill discounting, factoring, invoice discounting, block discounting (see Chapter 14 for details). Can you use any of these services in your business?

(h) GRANTS AND SUBSIDIES

Grants and subsidies are offered by national, regional and local government agencies covering, for example: subsidies on capital expenditure; construction of factories (standard or to your design) for you to rent; staff training grants; and a host of others. Those depend upon the type of buinesss, where it is located, the type of people employed, etc. The 'special offers' change about as frequently as those in a supermarket and it is impossible in a book to give a comprehensive and up-to-date list. Appendix 2 gives some guidance on how to obtain information about current offers and terms. Check whether any of these might apply to you. Check also how far you would have to move location to get a better offer.

If you are not sure whether some suggestions apply to you, ask your accountant or solicitor. When you have examined them all, list those ideas which might be adopted and estimate the reduction in capital for each. Make sure there is no contradiction or double counting.

This reduction in capital needs is rarely sheer profit. There is usually a price tag, in terms of increased expenditure or reduced income. Often there are other implications, e.g. restrictions on freedom, less attractive working conditions, narrower choice of suppliers and/or goods for sale.

Rank the items in order of capital saving, starting with the biggest, and mark against each the price tag in both financial and non-financial terms. This last step should highlight the 'best buys' and 'worst buys' and thus help you to decide which ones to adopt. Now work out revised total capital requirements and profitability.

Despite all your efforts, there may be a gap between capital needs and capital availability which you cannot bridge – yet. Resist the temptation to press on regardless, because this course is likely to cost you money, reputation and heartache. It is much better to work out how you are going to fill the gap. Get busy earning and saving more money, preferably in a way which gives you useful experience, e.g. by part-time work in the trade. At least make sure you employ the time profitably by acquiring more knowledge and improving your plans.

Presenting your case

Every successful entrepreneur has a streak of salesman in him. Businesses may differ in the degree of salesmanship needed but there is always a selling angle. The first serious test of your salesmanship is in persuading someone to put up money to back you.

First you must prepare your case. Thorough homework is essential since a case is like an iceberg: only 10 per cent is shown but an unseen 90 per cent is the base which supports it. For the sake of effective presentation, only one case may be presented, but a number of variations and contingencies must be worked out so that you can cope with questions.

The way you present your case depends upon your audience. Keep it simple and concentrate on those aspects which appeal to the interests and prejudices of the listener. When in doubt, it is better to over-simplify the main presentation, leaving details to be handled when answering questions.

Let us take the example of a bank manager, since this is the most common situation. Look at it his way: he wants to lend money, since this is how banks make a profit, but he has more borrowers than money to lend. Therefore he must discriminate in some way. He does this by eliminating all applicants whose schemes do not appear 'sound'. Then he allocates his funds to the most 'attractive' of the remaining schemes.

In making his judgement as to whether or not a proposition is 'sound', he must first decide on its *viability*, i.e. is it likely to be sufficiently profitable and survive long enough to service the loan? Second, he must decide on the *competence* of the borrower to run that particular business. Third, he is interested in the *security* offered, just in case his judgement is wrong, i.e. if the worst comes to the worst, can enough be salvaged to repay the loan? He judges 'attractiveness' in the same way.

Naturally the bank manager hopes you will be successful and that *your* growing turnover will increase *his* turnover. But it takes a lot of increased turnover to offset a few losses – so he is cautious. Moreover, he is well aware that his judgement is partly subjective, so the more figures you can show him, the more comfortable he feels. Knowing what he wants, you can present your case in a way which pleases him.

(a) *Describe your business* – what you are going to make or sell or offer as a service. If it is unfamiliar, it helps to show a sample or a photograph or sketch (*not* a technical drawing). If it is highly technical, think of a homely analogy which will help him to grasp it. You can't expect anyone – especially a bank manager – to lend money for something he doesn't understand.

(b) Show how much *fixed and working capital* you need, preferably as a neatly typed, concise table.

(c) Show your *target income and expenditure*, and the assumptions on which it is based, in the form of a neatly typed statement.

(d) Show your *cash-flow calculations*, month by month for the first 12 months, in the form of a table or graph (see Chapter 7).

(e) List the qualities required to run such a business, followed by a concise statement of the relevant *qualifications and experience* possessed by yourself, your partners (if any) and key staff (if important).

(f) Show your *market forecast* for the next few years as a table or graph – the total market in your territory and how you expect it to be shared between your competitors and yourself. If you have already obtained advance orders or contracts, show them to him.

If your proposition is sound and you have done your homework thoroughly, the presentation of the above information to your bank manager will go a long way towards convincing him that he ought to back you.

The photographs, statements, tables and graphs will greatly speed up your presentation and the bank manager's comprehension. You should aim to present the whole show in ten to fifteen minutes. Write out what you intend to say and then make brief notes to use during presentation. Get a long-suffering friend or relative to act the part of bank manager while you rehearse it until you feel confident.

The bank manager will probably not give you an answer off the cuff. He will want to think about it, check your credit rating and perhaps consult colleagues or Head Office. Leave a copy of your display sheets with him to think over. If your business is very technical, attach an explanation in technical language which he can show to the bank's experts for an opinion.

If the person you are approaching is not a bank manager, the same general principles still apply. Think about what that person wants to know about the proposition and about you. What aspects of the case will seem most important to him? Then structure your presentation accordingly.

You may be tempted to think that the above is an awful lot of trouble to take just to borrow some money. Is it really? Can you start your business without that money? And isn't starting a business very important to you?

Moreover, you will find that, once prepared, your presentation serves many purposes. You will find yourself repeating excerpts from it when talking to suppliers, customers and others. The way you roll off a lucid account of your business, complete with facts and figures – apparently impromptu – impresses your listeners no end. You exude self-confidence, which is good for business – and for your self-confidence.

CHAPTER 7

Getting off the Ground

Until they start their own business, few people appreciate what is meant by the 'loneliness of command'. You suddenly realize you have problems and no one to discuss them with. You will probably get lots of well-meant advice and much of it may be good. The real difficulty is that no one points out the gaps in this advice; you have to find these out for yourself.

Often it is not so much advice that is needed as a patient listener or 'sounding board' against whom to bounce ideas. If you are lucky, you have a spouse or good friend to fill this role but they may not always be around. You will notice this loneliness most in the early days because this is when you are adjusting your habits and work methods to fit the new situation. The purpose of this chapter is to discuss the early stages of getting your business under way, paying particular attention to ways of managing on your own.

Thinkbooks

The method which I devised to overcome loneliness was to use a series of 'thinkbooks'. At first this was just a loose-leaf book in which I put my random jottings so that I would not lose or forget them. As it grew, I found it convenient to divide it up into sections. Gradually it developed into six separate loose-leaf books entitled 'Ideas', 'Studies', 'Strategy', 'Action', 'Controls' and 'Review'.

It may sound a bit daft to talk to yourself but I found it made good sense to write to myself. You may prefer to arrange things differently but I shall describe how I use my thinkbooks.

IDEAS BOOK

This is for all the random ideas which come into my head at any time of day – new products, new markets, better methods, possible customers ... and so on. I may write just a few words or I may write several sentences, depending on the time available. Then when I am looking for a way of solving some problem, I have a 'trawl' through the book. It is amazing how often I find ideas I had forgotten about completely.

STUDIES BOOK

When I finish a study, I staple together all the working papers (done on loose leaves) and put them in this book. Often the calculations from one study save time on another.

STRATEGY BOOK

This contains all the papers relating to my Business Strategy. The development of this is described in Chapter 22.

ACTION BOOK

This contains all the papers relating to the Action Plan described later in this chapter and in Chapter 22.

CONTROLS BOOK

This contains all the papers relating to Business Controls, described in Chapter 13.

REVIEW BOOK

This contains all the papers relating to Monthly and Annual Reviews, which are described in Chapter 13.

Timing the start

Having decided to start a business, most people are impatient to get under way as quickly as possible. Before giving way to this impulse, however, you should ask yourself, 'When is the best time for *me* to start?'

Many businesses are seasonal, e.g. fireworks, ice cream, tourism, winter clothing, cricket gear. Since cash flow is a problem for many entrepreneurs, it may be better to commence trading at a time of high sales rather than low sales. So find out how the volume of sales might be expected to fluctuate, month by month, over the year.

There may of course be good reasons for starting at another part of the seasonal cycle. For instance it may be much easier or cheaper to obtain premises or equipment out of season. You may be inexperienced and wish to build up your expertise during quiet trading conditions so that you are better able to cope when the rush comes.

You should also consider the current state of the 'business cycle'. Many branches of industry and commerce go through a sequence which, at the risk of over-simplification, may be described as (a) business booms; (b) firms expand capacity and new firms enter the trade; (c) over-capacity leads to price-cutting; (d) profit margins decline and some firms leave the trade (voluntarily or by bankruptcy); (e) business picks up again and reduced capacity leads to rising profit margins; (f) business is booming again – back to (a).

Typically, such a cycle lasts about four years but you cannot count on this, since it is subject to other influences, such as political and economic crises. Nevertheless, it is worth a thought since it is obviously more attractive to commence trading at a stage (a) in the cycle, rather than stage (d). Of course, if you have adequate resources, stage (d) might give you the chance to buy an existing business at a bargain price.

A further obvious factor is your financial situation. You may have money due to be paid on a future date, e.g. from an endowment policy. Conversely, you may have been offered attractive voluntary redundancy terms, an offer which you must exercise before a certain date. In both cases, you need not start your business immediately you get the money, since it can be invested temporarily. In the latter case, however, lack of a job may oblige you to begin at once.

Finally you should consider your tax position. If you cease work late in the tax year, you may get a substantial PAYE tax refund.

Cash-flow calculations

Once you have decided upon the timing of the start, you can study the cash flow. The calculation of 'income and expenditure' described in Chapter 4 shows how the business looks once it is established but most businesses pass through a less profitable, or even loss-making, period before they are established. You should try to estimate how deep the trough is to check that your resources survive it.

This time, rule your sheet of paper into thirteen columns, one for the list of items and twelve consecutive monthly columns, starting with the month when you first pay out a significant amount of money. (This could be before the business is operating). For cash-flow purposes, it is irrelevant whether it is a capital or an operating expense. All that matters is what money flows out, what money flows in, when the flow takes place and what the balance is at any moment.

Put under each month the volume of sales expected for that month, i.e. the amount you expect to sell, whether or not it is paid for that month. Be realistic about this, since it may well be zero or very low for the first few months. Rule a thick line under this so that it is not added in to subsequent totals.

The first heading on the list is 'Preliminary Expenditure'. Under this go items such as: company formation; licences; legal fees; accountant's fees; consultant's fees; market research; design fees. Put against these items the estimated amounts under the months when you expect to have to pay the bills.

The second heading is 'Capital Expenditure'. This will include all the items mentioned in Chapter 4, such as obtaining and fitting premises, buying and installing equipment, obtaining the initial stock.

The third heading is 'Operating Expenditure'. The items will be those already mentioned in Chapter 4 but the payments are probably not the same each month, nor will they all start in the same month. Unless you are sure that you will receive credit from your suppliers, you had better assume cash on delivery.

Add up all the above items under each month to obtain the total 'Cash flow out' for that month.

The next heading is 'Business Income'. This will comprise payments by customers and any other sources of businesss income. The problem here is to judge when you will actually be paid. If you have a shop with cash sales, there is no problem and you can enter the same figure as the 'sales' at the top of the column. Where you invoice on delivery or at the end of the month, with payment due within thirty days, it is less easy to decide. You will probably have to adopt a formula such as 25 per cent paid in the month sold, 50 per cent the next month, 25 per cent the month after.

The final heading is 'Other Income' which comprises all other sources of income such as redundancy payments, ex-gratia payments, tax refund, loans, etc. The amounts and timing of some of these may be difficult to judge but do your best and, when in doubt, be conservative. Finally, put an item under this heading in the first month for 'Starting balance' which is your best guess of the amount you will have available in cash, bank balance, building society account, etc. at the beginning of the first month.

Add up all the items under the above two headings to obtain the total 'Cash flow in' for each month.

Now put the heading 'Summary'. The first line is 'Business balance', obtained by subtracting, for each month, the 'Total cash out' from the 'Total cash in'. If the answer is negative, put brackets around it. This is the convention adopted now that accountants have discovered that a photocopy machine cannot distinguish between red and black ink.

A second line is 'Domestic balance'. Put down for each month the appropriate figure taken from the domestic budget statement worked out as described in Chapter 4. Again put negative figures in brackets. The third line is 'Overall balance', obtained by adding together the 'Business balance' and the 'Domestic balance' for each month, watching the brackets and inserting them where necessary.

The fourth line is 'Cumulative overall balance' and is obtained as follows: For the first month, repeat the figure given on line 3. For the second month, take the figure on line 4 for the first month and add to it the figure on line 3 for the second month, watching your negatives and positives. For the third month, take the figure on line 4 for the second month and add to it the figure on line 3 for the third month. Repeat this for the remaining months.

Now sit back and study line 4, which shows the trend of your cash balance during your first twelve months. Are you lucky enough to remain positive throughout? Or do you drop into brackets in one or two months? If so, what are you going to do about it? Can you change the timing of some of your expenditure or should you start on a different scale? Do you need more working capital than you thought? If so, how and where do you get it?

Worst of all, do you drop into brackets and stay there, perhaps with a mounting deficit as the months pass? If so, you have probably not picked a winner. There is a limit to what can be achieved by juggling the timing of expenditure, so try repeating the exercise with your second choice of business.

You may not find cash-flow calculation easy if you have not done it before but it is vital, not only at the start but throughout your business career. You must master the technique because, in the short term, it is your cash flow which dictates what you can and cannot do and when you can do it. It may seem hard to 'guess' the amount and timing of some cash flows but it gets easier with practice and you gradually develop a 'feel' for what is likely to happen.

Effective planning

There are a hundred and one (or more) things which have to be done to start a business. You can just do them as the thought strikes you and the need arises and, if you are lucky, the business gets going – after a fashion. But if you want to make sure your business will be successful, you cannot afford to leave so much to chance. You must plan.

To make an effective plan you must combine four elements: (a) the jobs to be done; (b) the order in which they must be done; (c) the times when they must be started and completed; (d) a control system to check results. There is a very good technique for blending these together in a major project, viz. *network analysis*. You may have heard of this under one of its other names, e.g. arrow diagram, critical path analysis, Programme Evaluation and Review Technique (PERT). If you have had previous experience of this method, you may wish to use it.

Unfortunately it is not an easy method as it is rather time-consuming to set up so, if it is unfamiliar to you, it is probably better to use the simpler technique of *bar charts*. For starting a small business this is likely to be just as effective and is much easier to understand and use.

A bar chart is a sheet of paper or a board, ruled with horizontal lines – one for each job – and a number of vertical columns. The jobs to be done are listed down the left-hand vertical column. Each of the other vertical columns represents a consecutive period of time, anything from a day to a year. Against each job a thick horizontal line or 'bar' is drawn through the appropriate vertical column(s) to show when you plan to do that job. (There are many types of 'planning board' for sale on the market if you don't want to make one yourself.)

Begin by drawing up a list of 'jobs to be done'. You will find it helpful to collect these under a number of headings such as: finance, supplies, workplace, transport, staff, insurance, prices, advertising, etc. The number of headings is not critical but it is usually convenient to have between ten and fifteen. Take a separate sheet of paper for each heading.

Most of the jobs to be done are probably discussed somewhere in this book. Read through the book carefully and jot down under the appropriate heading those items which are mentioned in the text or which occur to you as you read. If in doubt, write it down. You should only omit items which are already done or which you are certain do not apply to your business.

It is easier to spot when something is missing if you group related items together, hence the headings, but do not agonize too much over the classification since this is a waste of time. The important thing is to get every item down somewhere. Now look at your lists and rearrange them if necessary. You may want to subdivide some groups and combine others. You may want to choose some new heading to which you transfer jobs from other groups.

It is useful to give each job a code number. The best way is to give a letter to each heading and a number to each job coming under it. For instance, A4 might be 'remortgage home' and D2 'hire van'. Such a system allows you to add new items under the appropriate heading as they arise.

The time scale must now be chosen. Frequently this start-up plan comes to an end when you open for business but you may prefer to continue it for a further month or two. Whatever end date you decide, the difference between this and the present determines the duration of your plan. You need then only decide upon the time interval for each vertical column to calculate how many columns you need. In practice it is usually most convenient to let each column represent a month in the overall plan and a week in the action plan.

You can now begin to draw up your *overall plan*. You will probably have so many jobs that you need to spread them over several sheets, one or more headings to each, but the time scale must be the same on all. Taking each job in turn, draw a (pencil) line back from the latest finishing date permitted by your business start-up target to the earliest starting date allowed by your cash flow.

Once you have done this for all jobs, they must be cross-checked and adjusted to match up starting and finishing dates. For instance, you cannot fit out your workplace until you gain possession and you should not print company stationery until the company is formed. The corrected pencil lines can now be filled in with coloured ink or plastic strip to produce your 'bars'. This plan meets points (a), (b) and (c) of the requirements. Point (d) can be met by marking up the actual progress on each job in ink of a different colour.

The *action plan* is derived from the current month of the overall plan. Pick out those jobs which require action this month and work out a detailed programme to give a balanced workload, week by week. The same coloured ink or strip technique can be used to show actual weekly progress versus plan. Setting up the action plan each month provides a good opportunity to review progress on the overall plan and to indicate when revision of the plan may be needed.

Working methods

There are several reasons for studying your working methods before starting the business. Firstly, your methods should dictate the equipment you buy and the way you install it – not the other way round. Once heavy machinery is concreted in, it may be too expensive to change it. You may then have to adapt your methods to fit the layout instead of installing equipment to suit the best work method.

Secondly, your working methods should determine the kind of people you hire, the skills and experience you look for at recruitment and the training you give them. It can be difficult and expensive these days to pay off staff. Even if you still use them, they may not be happy working at a job which is different from what they were led to expect when engaged. The real danger is not that they leave, but that they stay on and grumble.

Thirdly, you have more time to think before you start than after you have started. This may seem strange to many people in the throes of preparing to start a business but it is true. You may of course be very busy just now but the time pressures are less acute. You don't have deliveries to make tomorrow. You don't have staff sitting doing nothing – with the timeclock ticking up – while you work out what they should do and how they should do it.

Admittedly there are many jobs you cannot do until you have actually started. All the more reason for doing as much as possible beforehand of jobs like the following:

- if it is important that staff use a particular method for certain jobs (e.g. for safety reasons), write down methods for these and put them in a loose-leaf book for easy reference (see Chapter 19);
- devise your business control systems and set up any graphs or wall charts needed (see Chapter 13);
- devise your stock-control system, write down the method and set up the system before materials begin to arrive (see Chapter 11);
- work out the physical layout of your stores and install shelving and bins (see Chapter 11);
- set up your book-keeping system, in conjunction with your accountant, and train whoever will look after it (see Chapter 14);

- devise your filing system for purchasing, sales, general correspondence, staff records, etc. and write down how it is to be used (see Chapters 13, 14, 16);
- if you expect to have repetitive correspondence, draft a number of standard letters which can be used as a model by your typist.

I should perhaps add that the above are not just the product of armchair imagination. They are based on personal experience of starting up several new projects – some small and some large. Establishing such an 'infra-structure' of frequently used methods in advance greatly reduces the number of unforeseen hitches and snap decisions required during the actual start-up.

CHAPTER 8

Professional Advice

In starting a business, you will inevitably encounter problems which are outside your previous experience. Some people 'soldier on' or 'play it by ear' or 'press on regardless' or employ whatever cliché they prefer to describe a blind venture into the unknown. Sometimes it works and sometimes it doesn't. One can collect a few scars this way and pay for some expensive lessons – whether one learns or not.

Others rush from one 'expert' to another, receiving expensive and perhaps conflicting advice. Some problems are solved but others may be created from the side-effects of the advice tendered.

Still others adopt a third way, which is to learn how to analyse problems not previously encountered and to judge when to apply DIY methods and when to use experts. They learn how to choose the right kind of experts and how to employ them effectively. The purpose of this chapter is to help the reader follow this third way – to use experts wisely.

Your 'three wise men'

There are three experts who are needed by everyone starting a business – a bank manager, accountant and solicitor. They are professional in every sense of the word and your relationship with them must be professional. This does not mean you cannot become friends. It means they do not *have* to become your friends – so long as you respect them and treat them in a way which makes them respect you.

Most of the experts you employ will be used only intermittently and possibly at long intervals. Your contact with these three is, however, likely to be frequent and fairly regular. The better they get to know you and your business, the better the quality of the advice they can provide and so you should not chop and change your 'three wise men'. Nevertheless, if you find at an early stage that you are unable to establish a good working relationship, you should not hesitate to change. Once you find someone satisfactory, stick to him.

It is a mistake to treat these three as 'trouble-shooters' whom you consult only when in a jam. When you see them on a specific business matter, take the opportunity to bring them up to date about how the business is going in general and your plans for the future. Do not allow too many months to elapse without seeing them and, if necessary, make an appointment to see them for a general up-dating session. In this way, they gain a better understanding of your business needs and of you as a person, which enables them to give a better service. From time to time they may be able to give you early warning of developments which might affect you.

It goes without saying that, if you are to take them into your confidence in this way, you must feel you can trust them. Professional competence is essential but it is not enough. If you lack this feeling of trust in one of these three advisers, you must change him for someone you can trust.

Other specialist advisers

There are a number of other specialist advisers whom you will need from time to time. For instance, you will almost certainly need a good *insurance broker*. In addition to the obvious things like property, fire and theft, car insurance, life and accident insurance you may also need cover against employers' liability, product liability and perhaps professional indemnity. You may also want advice on employee and self-employed pension schemes. Few, if any, insurance companies have a complete range of policies which are ideal for every purpose. Unless your needs are simple, therefore, it is better to deal with a reputable broker who can select from the policies offered by several insurers a package that best meets your needs.

If you have any involvement with property, you are likely to need a *surveyor*. Don't try to economize on this by doing it yourself or by assuming that if the building society approves it must be all right. You need your own man to examine the property and give you a detailed report. There may be times when you pay him for a survey which results in your not taking on a property. This is not a waste of money because his report has probably saved you thousands of pounds. If any extensive building work has to be done, it is usually worth getting him to supervise. A surveyor is also needed if you want to check your rating assessment and, if you decide to challenge it, he is the best person to argue your case with the local authorities.

Property negotiations will also bring you in contact with *estate agents*. But if you are a prospective buyer or tenant, remember that the estate agent works for the owner. However nice he may seem to you, he is on their side because they pay him.

Many small businesses are reluctant to employ an *advertising agent*. This reluctance may stem from modesty or, alternatively, from over-confidence in their own abilities or perhaps from fear that they will be talked into spending more than they need or can afford. If your advertising budget is big enough, you should seriously consider using a regular agent because there is a lot of expertise behind the brash front. The owner of a business is rarely good at designing his own advertising.

The above are only a few of the more common specialists used by businesses. There are, however, other sources of help which are free or modestly priced, e.g. suppliers, higher educational institutions or the Small Firms Information

Centres. Even if they cannot answer your specific question, they are often able to point you in the right direction. Further details of these and other sources of help are given in Appendix 2.

How to choose them

The best way to choose any professional adviser is the same as when picking a doctor or dentist, i.e. on the recommendation based on personal experience of someone you trust. If this method is not possible, what then?

The first advisers you should appoint are your 'three wise men' – bank manager, solicitor and accountant. It is best to start with your bank manager. If you have had a bank account at a local branch and had mutually satisfactory relations for several years, this is the obvious starting point. Make an appointment to talk to the manager, explain what you intend to do and ask if he is happy to open a business account for you. At the same time, weigh him up and decide whether you can work with him.

If your personal account is at a branch too far away, ask that branch manager to give you an introduction to the local branch manager, then proceed as described above.

If you do not have a bank account, ask your friends about the local banks then decide which one is most suitable. The best course of action then is to persuade someone who is already a respected customer of that bank to introduce you personally to the manager.

The most difficult situation is where you already have a local bank account but relations are poor, for whatever reason. It is probably best, in that case, to choose a new bank and arrange an introduction to the manager through an existing good customer. Explain your project and ask if he will open a business account for you. If he is willing, he will probably ask you to transfer your personal account to his branch. If he is not willing, try somewhere else. The thing to watch is not to transfer your personal account until you have the business account fixed up.

The choice of bank manager has been dealt with in some detail, since he is the 'anchor man' in your professional advisory team. If you do not already have an accountant or solicitor you can approach the professional societies (see Appendix 2), explaining the nature and scale of your business and the professional services required. They will usually give you several names in your area. These can be discussed with friends who may have had experience of them. If you are still unsure, talk it over with your bank manager.

Similar methods will be used in finding other types of specialist, viz. consulting friends, existing professional advisers and, if necessary, the appropriate professional society (see Appendix 2). Although frowned upon, or even forbidden in some professions, practitioners in others are allowed to advertise, so study the Yellow Pages, local papers and trade press. Whatever source you use to find names, try to get one or more opinions on a particular specialist before engaging him.

How to use them

One of the more difficult tasks in business is handling an expert in a field in which you have no experience. The need for specialist advice in a business can arise at any time but is particularly prevalent at the beginning – just when you have least experience in coping with them. Small wonder that the attitude of entrepreneurs can range from constantly looking over the specialist's shoulder and arguing about everything he does, all the way to giving him carte blanche and being afraid to question anything.

At first sight it may seem difficult to generalize about how to treat such people. Quite an elaborate protocol is laid down by some professions, whereas others operate in an aura of high-pressure salesmanship. Nevertheless, there are certain steps which are common to the use of all experts.

The first step is to be quite clear in your mind what you want him to do in terms, not of how he does it, but of the result you want. You should really do this before you engage him since there are sub-branches of specialism in every field of expertise and a clear picture of the objective helps to get the right kind of expert.

Having chosen the expert, it is necessary to work out jointly the work he should do. Your contribution is to state clearly the objective you want to achieve; the expert's contribution is to suggest alternative methods, point out side-effects which might arise and give a rough indication of time-scale and cost. Having agreed upon a course of action, the expert should confirm this in writing, stating what he promises to do and when, whether he offers any guarantees and the basis of his charges.

If you are not handling the job yourself, you should appoint someone on your staff to act as 'contact' with the specialist, to provide information and assistance and to keep you informed. Periodic progress meetings should be held with the specialist to sort out any snags which arise. On completion, you should hold a brief post-mortem with members of your staff and perhaps the specialist. The object of this is not to apportion the blame for anything which went wrong but to see what can be learned about how to handle specialists in future.

What does it cost?

Some professional advisory services are free, as indicated above, but in most cases they have to paid for. The methods used for assessing fees are of bewildering variety. Your *bank manager* will not, as a rule, charge for time spent by himself or his assistants in discussing your affairs, although there are rumours that some banks may begin to do so. There are, of course, the usual bank charges and there is likely to be a charge made for drawing up a loan or overdraft agreement. Moreover, if he obtains advice for you from the bank's experts, there will probably be a fee.

Your *solicitor* may charge in several ways. For some common jobs, e.g. conveyancing of property, the Law Society lays down a scale of charges, based on the value of the property. For some other jobs the Law Society sets a fixed fee. In most other cases the solicitor fixes the fee, which is probably based on the time he spent on it plus the amount of correspondence and telephoning involved. If he is doing a lot of work for you, it may be worth agreeing mutually on an annual retainer to cover certain services.

Your *accountant* may work on an agreed annual fee if the work is straightforward, such as preparing and auditing your annual accounts and/or preparing your tax return. If your affairs are complicated or if you consult him on other matters, he will probably charge you a fee based on the time it takes.

An *estate agent* will usually charge the seller of a property on a scale of charges related to the selling price. For administration of property, he will probably charge a percentage of the rental plus certain expenses. For examining a property, some *surveyors* use a scale of charges based on the value of the property. Others may have a fixed fee or base their charges on the time taken.

Insurance brokers and *advertising agents*, on the other hand, do not charge the user for their services. They make their living by receiving a commission from the insurance company which issues the policy or from the publication which prints the advertisement. In both cases, however, if you ask them to do special work, you are likely to be charged for it.

Once you ask a specialist to do something for you, you become liable to pay whatever fee he charges. If you think the fee is too high you can, in some cases, appeal to his professional society to assess whether the charge is reason-able. Alternatively, you can apply to the High Court or County Court to have the bill 'taxed', i.e. you ask the court to decide the charge.

There is no guarantee that these measures will reduce the bill. In fact you may end up paying the original bill plus the costs of querying it. It is only common sense, therefore, to find out what something is going to cost before you commit yourself. At that point you can still decide not to have the job done or to find another, cheaper specialist.

Take care, however, lest the 'cheaper' specialist costs you more in the long run. If you need to engage a specialist because of your ignorance about a particular subject, you depend heavily upon the advice given. You cannot afford incompetence, however cheap.

CHAPTER 9

Choosing a Workplace

In many businesses, the choice of a workplace is one of the most critical decisions made by the entrepreneur. Moreover, this is a decision which usually has to be made before the business gets under way, so you may be very inexperienced at the time you make it. In this chapter we shall discuss the factors which influence the choice, so that you don't overlook the ones which matter to *your* business.

You may be thinking about moving to another district. If the local market is too small for your business or suffers from over-competition, such a move may be unavoidable. If you can get substantial financial help from government or local authorities, it may be attractive. In the absence of such compelling reasons, you should hesitate to move from a district where you have friends and relations to help you and where you know whom to contact to get things done. Even if you have difficulty finding a workplace, it may be better to persevere locally than move to another place where you are friendless and an 'incomer'.

The importance of location

The first factor to consider is *location*. For example, a newsagent or tobacconist shop will usually do much better in a busy main street than in a quiet back street. Even in a main street, one side may be busier than the other. Perhaps it is better paved, it may be sunnier or more sheltered in bad weather, or the other shops on that side attract people. The position of a bus stop, car park or railway station can also make some parts of a street more favourable than others.

You can quickly learn something about the importance of

location by carrying out the following simple experiment. Pick a shop of the type and size you have in mind and count the number who enter it in, say, an hour. Then repeat the process with three or four similar shops in different locations at the same time of day. Try to work out why one shop is busier than another. You may be surprised to find how great the difference is between the busiest and the quietest.

Obviously location is not the only thing that matters. An attractive appearance and pleasant staff can go some way towards offsetting a less favourable site but only some way. Landlords usually have a shrewd idea of the value of a good location but it may be a bad bargain to choose a poor location just because the rent is low. On the other hand, if your business does not need a 'good' location, it is sheer extravagance to pick an expensive site.

What do you need?

Before you go shopping around for a workplace, you should decide what you are looking for. How much floor space do you need for working in, for office accommodation, for sanitary and other facilities? Be particularly careful in estimating your needs for storage of raw materials, components, work in progress and finished goods, since this is often the biggest space-user. How much of your space needs to be under cover and how much in the open? Does the yard space need to be protected by a security fence?

Before deciding on your area, it is a good idea to examine a number of similar businesses. Not only will this give you a rough measure of your needs but you can get ideas to copy in laying out your space – and faults to avoid. As well as looking at the space, you can also learn a lot by talking to employees.

Does it matter whether the space is square, long and narrow or irregular? Must the building possess any special features, e.g. high ceiling, strong walls for mounting equipment or heavy shelves, reinforced floors, good sound or heat insulation? How much natural light and ventilation do you need? What size should the doors be? Does the building have to be in a very good state of repair?

There are not many small firms which need *rail access* these days. If you do, this will limit considerably your choice of sites. Consider, however, whether it is advantageous to be near a goods depot or railway station.

You will almost certainly require *road access*. How important is this? Close access to a motorway junction may cut several miles off every delivery you make. Check with your suppliers what size and type of vehicles they use at present and whether they plan any changes in the near future. How much space is needed for turning? Will there be any problems caused by width, length, height or weight of vehicles, whether your own or those of suppliers, customers or services? How much parking space will be needed for cars and goods vehicles?

What services do you need for *water* and *sewage*? Do you anticipate any *waste disposal* problems – gases, dusts, liquids or solids? What type of *power supply* do you need? Do you need *telephone* or *telex* facilities? What is the realistic time for installing these in your area? Do you need special *postal* facilities? Will your business create *noise* or *traffic* problems if located in certain districts?

Having worked your way through these questions, you are now able to draw up a checklist to use when evaluating possible properties. It is easier to compare these if you draw up your list in two parts: (a) *essential features* which the premises must possess or which can be installed; (b) *desirable features* which you would like but which can be omitted – at a price.

Fixing it up

It may seem premature to think about fixing up the work-place before you have found it, but this is not so. You should have at least a rough idea of how you intend to fix it before you start looking at possible premises, since this can influence the relative attractiveness of the alternatives available.

As a first step, it is usually advisable to decide upon the layout of the equipment, fixtures and fittings. Not only is this often the major factor in deciding the floor space you need but, once fixed, the layout largely determines your working methods, how much walking the staff have to do and how much you have to handle materials. This can influence the number of staff needed for a particular turn-over, the amount of handling equipment needed and perhaps even the capacity of the workplace. The position of equipment also affects the cost of running cables and piping.

The ideal layout from one viewpoint may not be the best from another. It may therefore be necessary to compare several alternative layouts until the best compromise is achieved. This exercise will give you a 'feeling' for the most convenient shape of premises, the best location for doors and windows and indicate the relative financial importance of the different features.

The style and quality of decoration will be dictated mainly by the nature of your business and your class of market. Before you start looking at premises, you need some idea of the standard you will aim for and how much you can afford to spend to achieve it. You must also consider the extent to which you will engage contractors to do the work and how much you intend to do with your staff and/or yourself.

It is helpful to find out beforehand roughly how much it will cost for the various types of work – building modifications, joinery, painting, electrical, plumbing, etc. Armed with this information, you can then make a quick assessment of whether a particular premises is within your range or not before you spend too much time on it.

Security v. flexibility

In starting a business, one has to meet two requirements which are often in conflict – security and flexibility. Having got a business going nicely in a particular location, you do not want to be forced to move. On the other hand, if the original site becomes no longer suited to your needs – for whatever reason – you want to be free to move. In practical terms, this often boils down to the age-old question, 'Should you buy your workplace or rent it?'

Very often there is no simple, clear-cut answer because it is not a simple problem. It may involve not only security and flexibility, but also capital availability and other factors. You must weigh the pros and cons and decide what suits you best. In making your decision, you should consider the following:

Buying is favoured when:
• you have ample capital available;
• an attractive mortgage is offered;
• you are taking over an established, going concern;
• you have experience of the type of business;
• you know the location well;
• you intend to live on the premises;
• the business is expected to grow slowly.

Renting is favoured when:
• capital is scarce;
• it is difficult to get a mortgage;
• the business is novel;
• you are inexperienced in this type of business;

- there has not previously been such a business in that location;
- if successful, expansion may be rapid.

A third choice exists, namely leasing. This is not as permanently binding as buying but offers more security than renting. Be cautious, however, since it is sometimes more difficult to sell a lease than a freehold.

Occupation of a particular property does not necessarily confer the right to do as you wish. Local authorities have power to divide their area into zones for specific purposes – agriculture, industry, housing, etc. – and you may not, for example, run a manufacturing business in an agricultural or housing zone. When new zones are created, existing businesses are sometimes permitted to continue, but this permission may not be passed on to a new proprietor. Nor may an existing one be permitted to extend the premises.

Apart from local authority regulations, the deeds of ownership or the tenancy contract may prohibit the conduct of certain types of business. There are also licensing regulations which apply to certain types of business (e.g. public houses) and the licence is not automatically passed on to the new occupant. When premises are used for a different purpose (e.g. hotel, food store), new regulations come into force and the authorities concerned may demand changes in the building structure or layout.

Before committing yourself to a particular property, whether as owner or tenant, you must make sure that you will be allowed to carry on the type of business you have in mind. This means that you, or your solicitor, must study the district council plans, approach the relevant licensing authorities and check for the existence of any restrictive covenants on property which interests you. You should also find out what conditions might be imposed should you wish to extend the premises.

Timing

In Chapter 7 we discussed how to choose the best time to start the business. When do you need to get the premises to fit in with these plans? If you get it too soon, you are laying out capital or paying rent earlier than you need; if you get it too late, you may jeopardize your plans. What should be taken into account in deciding the ideal occupancy date?

First, there is the paperwork. You cannot register your company or your business name until you know the address you want to register (although the registered office of a company need not be where the business is conducted). You cannot, in general, apply for licences or permission to trade without giving the business address. So you need to find out how long it will take to complete whatever formalities are necessary for your particular business.

Second, there is the fixing up. This depends partly upon the condition of the property you choose. It also depends partly upon the delivery time of special equipment. Indeed you may need to take a chance and order key items of equipment, in the hope that you will have somewhere to put it by the time it comes.

Third, there is the time which may be needed to 'set up' the business before you begin trading. In a selling business you have to order and lay out your goods for sale. In a manufacturing business you must get a stock of raw materials and components and perhaps make a selection of finished articles for demonstration or display. In many businesses, staff will have to be engaged and trained.

How to find it

There is no single source of information on business premises and you must be prepared to do a lot of library work, telephoning and travelling around. Luck undoubtedly comes into it but luck can be stimulated by intelligent initiative. In short, you must follow up a wide range of possible sources and see what comes up.

Most property changes hands through the medium of business transfer agents or estate agents who specialize in commercial or industrial property. You can find ones in your district in the Yellow Pages and for the cost of a few phone calls, you can soon find which are likely to be of use to you and what is currently on the market.

Some agents operate nationally or regionally, instead of on a local basis, specializing in a particular type of business. Their advertisements can be found in the appropriate trade journals. Most trade journals also carry advertisements of businesses for sale. The local press usually contains advertisements of property available. A session in the reading room of a good public library will soon show you which publications are likely to be useful. It is worth buying or consulting these regularly during your hunting season.

Your local district council is well worth a visit. Not only are they often considerable landlords but they know where all the local shopping centres and industrial estates are located, who owns them and who the agents are. Many authorities are now keen to encourage new enterprises in their district and will go to some lengths to help. Telephone your nearest Small Firms Information Centre (see Appendix 2) to see what help they can offer.

Ask your bank manager if he knows of any property available and if he can suggest any contacts. Visit local industrial estates (if you want industrial premises) and ask the people working there if they know of anything available. Ask suppliers (if you want a shop) if they know of anyone wanting to sell.

At first you should examine as many premises as possible to form an idea of 'normal' conditions and prices. Once this is gained, you can be more selective, using your checklist to eliminate the obviously unsuitable. Do not, however, stop searching until you have a contract signed for a suitable premises.

Counting the cost

Once you have found a particular premises which seems to be a serious possibility, you will want to have some idea of what it will cost to acquire, fix up and use before you commit yourself.

To buy it, you will incur some or all of the following expenses: solicitor's fees, agent's fees, surveyor's fees, mortgage deposit and mortgage expenses such as lender's surveyor's fees, mortgage indemnity insurance premium, entrance fees, etc. Ask the people concerned for an estimate of what their fees will be for that particular property, based on the asking price. You will also want to know the rate of mortgage repayment and annual payments such as property insurance.

If you are renting or leasing the premises, your expenditure pattern will be different. You will still incur solicitor's fees and perhaps agent's fees and surveyor's fees. You should also find out what your obligations will be as tenant or lessee for initial installations, decoration and maintenance and what will be undertaken by the landlord or lessor.

In addition to the expenditure arising from the acquisition of premises, you will also incur the cost of fixing it up for your purpose. Use the earlier part of this chapter to compile a list of the items which apply in your case. Estimate, as well as you can, the expenditure required in terms of: (a) initial outlay, (b) regular running costs, (c) periodic expenses such as redecoration or repairs.

You will now have a list of items of expenditure arising from various sources. This list should now be used in two ways. First you must decide which items should be treated as *capital* and which as *revenue*. You will probably need the help of your accountant in this, from whom you should also find out if any items are not tax-deductible. Your account-ant will also advise upon the rates to apply to capital ex-penditure to assess the *capital allowances* which will be allowable in your tax calculations. The second use of the figures is to work out the *cash flow*, month by month, during the period of securing and fitting out your workplace, using the method described in Chapter 7.

Making the choice

If you have discovered several possible workplaces, you have to choose the best. If none is best in every aspect, this can sometimes be difficult. The following method may be used.

Rule up a sheet of paper into several vertical columns, the first for listing criteria and then one for each premises. In the first column list the *essential features* from your checklist. Taking the first feature, write down your assessment of each premises according to the rating: excellent, very good, ac-ceptable, fair, bad. Do the same for the other features. Then list the *desirable features* and repeat the process. Then list the criteria *location, security, flexibility, timing* and rate each premises in turn. Now list the features *capital, revenue* and *cash flow* and rate the figures for each premises in com-parison with your budget.

Having thus prepared a concise table of the advantages and disadvantages of each premises, it should not be too hard to decide which is best. You must now consider whether the best (or only) one discovered so far is good enough for your purpose or whether you must keep on look-ing. The table should help you decide this too.

Working at home

Many a flourishing business has been started at home and you may decide to follow their example. It is certainly an excellent way to keep costs down, particularly if you are starting on a part-time basis. Not only does it save money, it also saves time, which can be equally important. If you work at home, it is usually possible to agree with the tax inspector that a proportion of your domestic expenses (e.g. heating, electricity, telephone, etc.) can be charged to the business.

Working at home should not stop you from being business-like, right from the beginning. Try to negotiate with the family for the exclusive use of one room for your business. If this is not possible, try at least to get part of a room and the undisturbed use of it for certain hours of the day.

Get a second-hand desk to work on and store your papers, so that you do not have to pack up every time the family wants to use the dining-room table. If you use the garden shed or garage as a workshop, it is probably worth fitting an extension from your telephone, so that you do not have to run through the rain every time you get a call.

Some of the earlier points in this chapter apply to the use of your own home for business. You should check whether there is anything in the deeds or tenancy agreement which prohibits you from carrying on a business. You should also check whether you need a licence or permission from the local authority.

A debatable point here is what constitutes a 'business'. If you are only doing paperwork at home and using the telephone, there is a fair chance of a blind eye being turned. But if you regularly conduct noisy operations in the garage or have a lot of vehicles coming to the house or parking in the road, your neighbours are likely to complain. If someone complains, the local authority is obliged to take action. Tact, common sense and good relations with your neighbours would appear to be the guiding principles.

CHAPTER 10

Buying a Going Concern

When you buy a going concern, you are buying time and buying experience. You obtain an immediate income instead of undergoing a period of low profits or even losses while getting established. It would be naïve to regard this as a trouble-free way of starting a business but you should have fewer troubles than if starting cold. If you are inexperienced, you may hope to keep the business ticking over along existing lines while learning, but you must expect to pay for this. The purpose of this chapter is to help you choose the right business and try to ensure that you do not pay too much for it.

Plan of campaign

The first step in your plan of campaign is to decide clearly what you want and the resources you have to obtain it. If you have done your homework as you worked through the previous chapters, you should be able to summarize this along the following lines: type of business; location; target net income; approximate turnover; cash available; borrowing capacity (in addition to that of the business purchased); when you want to take over.

There are other factors which may not be easily quantifiable but which you need to think through to at least a tentative conclusion. The question of renting v. buying the premises may be influenced by the presence or absence of living accommodation. Do you want – or are you willing – to live on the job? How far are you prepared to travel from your present home? Are you willing to move from your present home?

Have you got your own staff lined up or are you prepared to take over existing staff? Can you wait until you judge the qualities of the existing staff? Would you prefer some of the existing staff to continue while you learn the business? Do you want the existing owner to stay on for a handover or training period?

Have you decided what legal form (see Chapter 5) you want to adopt for your business? Have you any preference about the legal form of the business you buy? Remember that if you buy a company, you take over all the obligations of that company (debts, tax arrears, etc.) unless you make an agreement to the contrary.

Once you are clear in your mind about what you seek, you can start the hunt, using the methods described in Chapter 9. At first, you should look at anything remotely possible, just for the experience. Then as you gain confidence, you can become more selective and submit the more promising candidates to a preliminary screening.

Preliminary screening

You should not of course purchase, or promise to purchase, any business until it has been thoroughly vetted by your professional advisers. There is no reason, however, why you should not do some preliminary screening yourself. If you turn it down at this stage you will have saved the professional fees. You will also have gained experience and begun to build up standards against which to compare the business you finally buy.

Start to assess the business before you enter the premises. How conveniently is it situated for public transport? Does the surrounding area look prosperous or run-down? Is the outward appearance of the business well-maintained or neglected? How easy is it to park in the vicinity?

When you enter the premises, what are your first impressions? How are you greeted? You will of course have made an appointment, so look for signs of hasty tidying up or 'putting on a show'. Try to make as thorough an inspection as possible, including storerooms and outbuildings. Is the equipment modern and in good condition? Does any of the stock look as if it has been there a long time? Does the place look well-run? What is your opinion of any staff you meet or see? You may not see as much as you would like, if the owner has not told the staff he is selling, but do the best you can.

Since inspection may inspire questions, it is better to look first and talk later. During inspection and discussion, try to avoid criticism by word or gesture. Criticism often arouses antagonism which may complicate subsequent negotiation, or even cause the owner to refuse to sell it to you. Unless you decide on the spot that the business is 'not on', the best course is to collect as much information as possible then take it away and think about it.

Ask to see the books and pay particular attention to figures over the last three years for turnover, gross profit, net profit, overheads, outstanding debtors and creditors. If he does not produce the books, make a note of any figures quoted. If he tells you that the business is actually more profitable than the books show, because of a tax dodge, discount this. It may be true, but you should only accept what can be proved.

What price is the owner asking for the business and how is the total broken down into (a) premises, (b) fixtures and fittings, (c) stock, (d) goodwill? What is the basis for each of these four and will the owner accept a neutral valuation for (b) and (c)? Try to judge whether he is willing to drop his prices. How and when does he want to be paid?

Ask why he wants to sell the business and what he proposes to do afterwards. When does he want to leave and what handover or introductory period will he provide? Ask what changes are expected in the neighbourhood – house construction and demolition, factory openings and closures, local authority zoning plans. (You can find out these last by other means to check how truthful he is.)

Finally, agree on a date by which you will give him a decision. Do not be pushed into giving any rash promises since, at this stage of inexperience, snap judgements are likely to be wrong. Then go away and think about it. Make notes while impressions are sharp in your memory. If you are undecided, talk it over with your professional advisers.

Bringing in 'the heavies'

By the agreed date, you should have told the prospective seller either that the deal is off or that you are interested, subject to a satisfactory report from your professional advisers. Now is the time to bring in 'the heavies'. The three advisers most commonly involved in a pre-purchase investigation are your solicitor, accountant and surveyor.

It is traditional, in professional practice, for the businessman to deal separately with each of these. This is not so in large companies, where it is common to appoint a team or 'task force' to work together. Such a method helps to avoid duplication of effort or errors of omission and so this is one case where the smaller business might well take a leaf out of 'big brother's' book.

Provided that their relations with you and with each other permit, call together a meeting of these three advisers and any others who may be involved. Give them a report of your preliminary investigation, both facts and impressions, and invite questions and comments. State clearly what your objectives are, i.e. the specification of the business you seek and the limits of time and money. Discuss and agree jointly what needs to be done, who should do it and the date by which it should be completed. In cases of disagreement, your decision should prevail, but the more that can be done by mutual agreement, the better the teamwork.

If they are unable to work as a team, for whatever reason,

you will have to discuss with each in turn to get their views on how to tackle the investigation. Then you will yourself have to make up the total list of jobs, allocate them and keep in touch with what each adviser is doing. It is a less satisfactory method but sometimes there is no alternative.

Broadly speaking, the purpose of the investigation is to enable the following questions to be answered.

PREMISES

Are there likely to be any difficulties in transferring the ownership or tenancy to you? Do you need permission to conduct the business on these premises and can you get it? Are the premises in a good state of repair? How much will it cost to repair and maintain them? Are they immediately suitable for your purpose or must they be modified? What additional services must be provided and how easy will this be? How long will the various changes take?

GOODWILL

What is the *true* profit of the business at present and in recent years? What changes in profitability can be foreseen? Is the present reputation of the business a liability or an asset? To what extent can goodwill easily be transferred (e.g. strategic location)? To what extent is goodwill not transferable (e.g. owner's personality)? Is the business heavily dependent upon a few large customers? How will the profits be affected if you take over? Are there any major problems and can you solve them? Are any large debts or taxes outstanding?

FIXTURES AND FITTINGS

Are these exactly what you need or do they have to be modified? In what condition are they? How much must be scrapped? How long will it take to get new equipment?

STOCK

How suitable is the existing stock for your purpose? Is any

of it unsaleable or unusable? Have you a disposal problem? How much is the total stock worth? How much of it do you want to keep? How long will it take to obtain new stock?

STAFF

Have you any obligation to continue to employ existing staff? Are they too many or too few for your purpose? Are there any key individuals whom you wish to retain? Are there any staff you do not wish to keep? How easy will it be to engage more staff? What is the state of morale at present? How do present salaries and conditions of employment compare with your intentions (see Chapter 16)?

You will probably not have sufficient time to investigate everything nor, perhaps, can you afford to do so. Your previous homework will tell you which are the most important things to you and your advisers can tell you how long each job will probably take. From this knowledge, you must draw up a priority listing of (a) what must be done at an early stage, (b) what is desirable to do, (c) what can be omitted without too much risk.

As the investigation proceeds, a picture will emerge of just how suitable that particular business is for you. If anything totally unacceptable comes to light, you will stop and withdraw immediately. Alternatively, the cumulative drawbacks may reach such a level that you decide to call it a day. On the other hand, you may decide that it meets your requirements, more or less, and be willing to buy it – if the price is right!

What is it worth – to you?

Before starting the buying process, you must decide what the business is worth and how much you are willing to pay for it; these two figures may be different. With the help of your professional advisers prepare an estimate in the following form. Rule up a sheet of paper with four columns, the first for items, the second headed 'Business Value', the third headed 'Additional Expenditure' and the fourth headed 'Credits'.

Write *Premises* in the first column and in Column 2 put what you consider to be a fair market value. This may be based on other property recently sold or rented in the district or on some formula recommended by your surveyor, taking into account the condition of the premises. In Column 3 list all the expenses you will incur in buying and making it suitable for your purpose, e.g. legal fees, survey fees, modifications, repairs, redecorations. In Column 4 put any credits you foresee arising, e.g. sale or rental of part of the premises not needed by you.

Now write *Fixtures and fittings* in the first column. There are two extreme views of the value to put in Column 2. The higher figure represents what it would cost to buy and install these with new or second-hand materials; the lower value is what the existing equipment would fetch if sold on the second-hand or scrap market. You will probably adopt some intermediate value which takes into account condition, suitability for your purpose, availability and delivery time for new equipment.

In Column 3 put the cost of modifying, repairing and redecorating the existing equipment plus the cost of buying and installing any new fixtures and fittings required. In Column 4 put an estimate of what you can get for any superfluous or scrap equipment, allowing for removal and selling expenses.

Entering *Stock* in the first column, you must put a value in Column 2. If you have the time and opportunity, the ideal way is to divide the stock into two parts. The part you want to keep is valued at the cost of replacing it at today's prices; the part you want to dispose of is valued at what you can get for a quick sale. Alternatively, you can value the total stock on each of the two bases and choose an intermediate figure, based on the relative proportion of the two parts. In Column 3 put the cost of additional stock needed to bring total stocks up to the level required. In Column 4 put the estimated proceeds of that part to be sold.

So far we have been trying to put a value on the *tangible assets* of the business, i.e. assets which consist of physical things such as buildings, equipment or stocks. A business which is already running has, however, some *intangible assets* which are not physical things you can see or touch. Assessing the value of these is more difficult but may be just as important.

The first is *Goodwill*, so put this in the first column. Briefly speaking, goodwill represents the difference between a collection of physical assets which produces an income and a similar collection which does not. It is an attempt to put a money value on the effort which the present owner, or his predecessors, has put into attracting and keeping a number of loyal customers. A method commonly employed is to say that goodwill equals x years' profits, but this does not help you to decide what value to put on x. You had better discuss this with your accountant.

One way of looking at it is to try to assess how long it would take you, starting from scratch, to build up the business to its present turnover. How many months or years would you have to incur running expenses while you progressed from nil turnover to today's turnover, to go from running at a loss to achieving the present profit level? Don't forget the loss of interest during this period on the original capital outlay and the salary you could have earned working for someone else. This approach should give you some feeling for the amount of money you should put down in Column 2.

In Column 3 put an estimate of what you expect to spend to protect this goodwill from the adverse effects of change of ownership. You may have to write to or call on existing customers to introduce yourself. You may have to advertise heavily for a time. Despite these efforts, there may be some drop in profits which – hopefully – will be temporary. Try to evaluate these things.

If you intend to sell off part of the business you buy, you may receive a payment for goodwill from the new buyer. This is probably the only item to be inserted in Column 4. You may feel that the present owner runs the business so badly that you are bound to do better. This may be true, but financial prudence dictates that you do not take credit for this until it has happened.

Goodwill represents the external asset, the customer, but there is also an internal asset – *Staff* – so put this in the first column. It takes time, money and effort to recruit, train and build up an efficient working team. What value would you put on the present staff? How much would it cost to recruit them? How long would it take to train them? Put a figure for this in Column 2.

On the other hand, some of the existing staff may not be an asset. Will the purchase result in your assuming responsibility for firing or pensioning off anyone? Will you incur liability for redundancy payments or retirement pensions? If so, put a figure in Column 3. There is probably no credit to insert in Column 4 unless you intend to run a professional football team.

Now add up the above figures. The total in Column 2 gives the best estimate of your advisers and yourself of the *value of the business to you.* If the price asked is greatly higher than your valuation, then probably no deal is possible. If the difference is reasonable or if the asking price is below your estimate, you may decide to purchase.

If the asking price is much below your valuation, take care! Check your calculations, particularly if a large part of your valuation relates to intangible assets. Does the owner know something you don't? Has the business been on the market a long time? Has the owner a particular reason for wanting a quick sale?

Before opening negotiations, there is one last check to be made. Most sellers expect to drop a bit on the original asking price. Try to guess, therefore, the price at which you might finally get the business. Add on the further expenditure you will incur (Column 3 total) and subtract any credits (Column 4 total). Is the net total more or less than you had planned to spend? If it is more than your budget, can you afford it? Do you *want* to afford it?

Negotiating the purchase

Do you intend to handle all the negotiations yourself? Or will you appoint one of your advisers to handle the deal on your behalf? Or will you break it into sections, each one handled by a different person? There is no universal best way; the decision will depend upon how experienced you are in negotiation, how experienced your advisers are and the complexity of the deal.

It may depend also upon how the owner wants it handled. The best course is probably to discuss it with your advisers and form an opinion as to the preferred method. Then you can approach the owner with your proposal but in the end you may have to compromise.

Whoever does the negotiating, *you* must decide on (a) the target price at which you would like to buy it and (b) the highest price you are prepared to pay. The tactics followed will depend upon the difference between these and the asking price. For instance, if the gap is small, you may seek to negotiate on the total price, concentrating your arguments on the weak points revealed by your evaluation.

If the gap is large, it may be more effective to break up the total price into the constituent parts – premises, fixtures and fittings, stock and goodwill – and try to negotiate a price for each which gives you the total price you seek. If the owner has given you a breakdown of his total, this will show you where to concentrate your big guns. It is probably wise not to reveal that you set any value on staff, although any liabilities towards staff may be used in argument.

Sometimes the owner resists very strongly dropping his price to a figure you can accept. Where this is due to pride, you may be able to persuade him to accept responsibility for some of the expenditure items in Column 3, such as repair and redecoration of premises or staff redundancy payments. In this way, you may be able to achieve what is effectively the financial result you want by means which are more acceptable to the owner.

Negotiations will not be confined to price alone. Terms of payment are also important. If only part of the payment need be made immediately, with the balance by instalments at no extra charge, this is equal to an interest-free loan, the value of which you can calculate. These instalments might depend upon specified minimum turnover or profit figures.

You may wish to negotiate a handover or introduction period before the business changes hands. You may also want to include a 'barring out' clause in the contract, i.e. debarring the owner from starting or being associated with a similar business within a certain area for a specified period of time.

It should not need saying but for safety's sake I shall say it: do not sign the contract until *all* your advisers have read it carefully and approved it.

CHAPTER 11

Equipment and Supplies

Over British industry as a whole, labour represents 60 per cent and materials 40 per cent of costs. These proportions obviously vary widely from one type of business to another, but there are few businesses where materials expenditure is unimportant. Even quite small businesses usually spend thousands of pounds each year on materials and, in many types of business, shrewd buying makes all the difference between profit and loss.

There are four main types of materials expenditure:

(a) *equipment, fixtures and fittings*, e.g. machinery, furniture, vehicles;
(b) *consumable materials*, e.g. stationery, lubricants, cleaning materials;
(c) *raw materials and components*, e.g. plastics, metal, electronic parts;
(d) *goods for sale*, e.g. articles bought for resale.

In your accounts, items in the first category are treated as capital expenditure and items in the remaining three as revenue expenditure. There are no standard terms for these different types of material so for convenience I shall use the term *equipment* to cover everything in class (a) and *supplies* for items in classes (b), (c) and (d).

Buying equipment

The first piece of advice to new businessmen thinking of buying equipment is – DON'T! Don't buy something unless you are absolutely sure you need it and will use it. No matter how cheap it may seem, an article is no bargain if you don't need it. If you use something only occasionally, borrow or hire it when you need it. If you use it regularly, rent or lease it. If you must buy it, get it second-hand or on HP. Outright purchase of new equipment for cash should be a last resort.

The reason behind this is that cash is scarce in most new businesses and should be conserved for those expenditures where there is no alternative (e.g. paying wages). Even if it isn't scarce, you should behave as if it is or you will waste it. Capital expenditure is a long-term commitment and it may be years before you get your money back on a piece of equipment – and all that time you have to give it house-room, service it, repair it and insure it. It may become obsolete or your needs may change before it has earned its keep, so avoid such commitments as far as possible.

When buying is inevitable, hunt for the 'best buy'. Compare the products of different manufacturers and compare prices from different suppliers. *Which* reports, published by Consumers' Association, sometimes show a price range of up to 30 per cent for the same article, so shop around and don't be afraid to haggle. If this embarrasses you, learn to overcome it because this must be your way of life as a businessman. A reputation as a hard bargainer is an asset. If you get a name for being a 'soft touch', there are unscrupulous people who will take advantage of it – and you have to deal with unscrupulous people some of the time.

Once you have got the price as low as possible, start haggling about the other terms. How much discount will they give for cash or payment within fourteen days? Alternatively, will they give you interest-free credit for, say, three months? Will they deliver and install it free? If you buy on HP, what are their terms? Will they give part-exchange on old equipment? What guarantees or free servicing can you obtain?

Buying supplies

When buying supplies you are working on a different time scale and you are buying repetitively. You may buy an item of equipment only once or at intervals of several years; you are buying supplies every week or month. Moreover, the price of an individual supply item is usually much less than that of an equipment item; it is the number of supply items which makes the bill significant. In addition, supply items have to be stored until they are consumed, used in manufacture or sold. These are the factors which cause you to adopt a different approach to buying supplies.

Consumable materials are a small proportion of expenditure in most businesses. This does not mean you should ignore them, but you should keep a sense of proportion. In the beginning you have probably not much idea of how much you will spend on consumable materials, so buy them locally at the best prices available and keep a detailed record of every item you buy, where you buy it and how much it costs.

After two or three months, add up the total and pick out the half-dozen biggest items. Does the scale of expenditure justify going further afield to find a cheaper source? Should you buy through mail order or go to a 'cash and carry'?

An alternative approach is to add up how much you are buying from each supplier. Can you negotiate a discount if you guarantee a minimum monthly order? If one supplier is willing to do this, how much business could you switch from the others to that one?

Unless the quantities are large and significantly better terms can be obtained elsewhere, it is better to stick to local suppliers for consumable materials. This is an inexpensive way of building up goodwill in the local community and may create business for you. In business terms, this is called *reciprocity*; in everyday terms, it is called, 'you scratch my back and I'll scratch yours'.

Raw materials and components warrant a lot of attention in most manufacturing businesses. Not only are they likely to be a significant item of expenditure, but faults may cause difficulties during your manufacturing process or give rise to complaints from your customers.

Materials and components are often bought according to a *specification*, i.e. a list of requirements which your purchase should meet. These may relate to fairly obvious qualities (e.g. colour, weight, thickness), qualities which must be assessed by scientific means (e.g. specific gravity, strength, chemical content), performance characteristics (i.e. ruggedness, accuracy, speed) or to more general guarantees of suitability for a particular purpose.

The specification used may be one of many thousands established by the British Standards Institute (BSI), well known for the famous 'kite' mark, or by a Trade Association. Alternatively, it may be one established by the supplier or, if you have enough 'muscle', by yourself.

Since quality costs money, you should not buy a higher quality than you need; on the other hand, the quality should not be so low as to cause trouble with your processes or customers. If there is a sliding scale of price v. quality, you should investigate whether a higher quality will reduce your processing costs or allow you to charge a higher price for your product.

In some cases you should *analyse* or *test* a sample of each delivery. If you lack the equipment or skill to do this, a sample can be sent to an independent laboratory, although this can be expensive. As a compromise, you may take a sample of each batch delivered and store it, only sending it for test should subsequent trouble arise.

Even the best of suppliers can sometimes make mistakes and so, whether you test or not, every delivery should be thoroughly examined on receipt to ensure that (a) it is addressed to you, (b) it has not been damaged in transit, (c) it is the material you ordered and (d) no items are missing.

Goods for sale represent the biggest single item of expenditure in many businesses and thus deserve a lot of attention. Your buying policy must be firmly based on your business strategy. Are you selling high-quality goods at a fair price or are you selling articles as cheaply as possible? Do you aim to keep a wide range in stock at all times or concentrate on a limited range of fast-selling items? Are you competing mainly on price or do you provide certain services, e.g. customer advice, free delivery, free installation? In short, what is your 'class of market'?

Your customers' buying habits will be reflected in your buying policy. If you want to build up a group of regular customers who look to you as the 'natural' place to buy certain goods, then you must build up a group of regular suppliers. If you aim to provide quickly those items not in stock, then you must find suppliers who provide a similar service. If you rely on attracting casual customers by large discounts, you must find sources of low-price goods.

Within the limitations imposed by the class of market chosen, as a beginner you should err on the side of too little rather than too much stock and too narrow rather than too wide a range. This does not mean you should open the shop with half-empty shelves. The shelves should be full but the storeroom should not. Such a policy helps, not only to conserve working capital but also to reduce losses caused by the buying mistakes you are bound to make through inexperience.

Keeping within your budget for opening stock, order as wide a range of goods as your policy dictates – but no more. Order the quantities that will sell within a reasonable period of time – but no more. Resist the blandishments of your suppliers' representatives – the 'massive discounts', the 'unrepeatable offers', the 'special lines'. If you are tempted to splurge, think about what else you must cut out to provide the money to pay for it.

Discount for quantity

Suppliers frequently offer discounts for large orders. This is partly because the cost of fulfilling an order is to some extent independent of the size of the order, partly to get you to buy more. From your point of view, the cost of ordering is also partially independent of size and, in principle, the less you pay for each article the greater should be your profit.

Increasing order size has, however, its disadvantages. Some goods are perishable and quickly become unusable or unsaleable (e.g. foodstuffs); some are subject to fashion and after a time can only be sold at a discount (e.g. clothing); others are subject to rapid technological change and may quickly be superseded by better/cheaper products (e.g. pocket calculators). In all cases, increasing your purchases means tying up more working capital. At best this means paying more interest and, at worst, the business can go bust because the cash flow dries up.

Deciding whether to place a larger order to receive a discount is therefore firstly a matter of calculating the saving in purchasing costs and comparing this with the increase in interest, storage and other costs. Then you must assess, as best you can, the effect of intangibles. Is the price likely to increase soon? Will interest rates change soon – in which direction – by how much? Will there by any losses through deterioration of goods in storage? Is a better or cheaper product likely to appear soon? Is demand likely to change during the storage period – up or down?

Where the answer is not clear-cut, the beginner should opt for the small order. It is sometimes possible to compromise by arranging a 'call off' order. You place a large order, which entitles you to a discount, but you have it delivered a bit at a time as you 'call it off'.

Sources of supply

Broadly speaking, there are three main types of supplier: manufacturer, wholesaler, retailer.

Manufacturers are frequently not interested in handling small orders and often impose minimum order quantities which are outside the scale of the new enterprise.

Wholesalers offer a range of goods from a number of manufacturers and carry stocks from which they can deliver quickly. If they impose a minimum order size, this may comprise goods from several manufacturers. These services must be paid for and, by and large, wholesalers' prices are higher than manufacturers' prices.

Retailers also offer a wide range of goods, although not necessarily more than that of wholesalers. The main facility they offer is convenience – they exist all over the country and most goods are available for immediate delivery. Although some retailers offer a 'trade discount' to certain classes of business customer, many do not. Even allowing for such discounts, retailers' prices are higher – sometimes considerably higher – than those of wholesalers or manufacturers.

Under these conditions, the new businessman tends to confine most of his buying to wholesalers. It is preferable to obtain the bulk of your supplies from two or three firms only. This allows you to place bigger orders with each, thereby obtaining more favourable terms and, perhaps, more frequent deliveries.

It is unwise to become too dependent on one firm because of the risk of strikes at that firm or in the distribution system. It helps if at least one main supplier is not too far away, so that you can collect materials yourself when needed urgently or during labour difficulties.

When choosing a main supplier, price although important is only one consideration. Credit terms also matter; in fact if you are counting on suppliers' credit as a source of capital to start your business, they are vital. Also important are reliability and promptness of delivery, range and quality of goods in stock and their 'reasonableness' in dealing with complaints.

Make a point of visiting the firm at the start of your business and at intervals thereafter. Although regular orders can be transmitted by post, telephone or sales representative, an established personal contact at a senior level can be most helpful in resolving any difficulties which might arise.

Storage and control

The cost of stocks and storage is sometimes underestimated. To begin with, there is the interest charge on the money tied up in stocks. To this must be added the capital invested in storage facilities, both buildings and open space, the interest on this and rent, rates and insurance. There is the time spent by staff in handling materials, both physically and on paper. Finally, there are stock losses through damage, deterioration and theft.

There are two keys to reducing stocks and storage cost: good *storage facilities* and efficient *stock control*.

Good storage facilities need not be expensive. What is needed is *good visibility* and *good protection*. One of the best ways of keeping tabs on stock is for the boss to inspect the store every day. The more visible the stock is, the more easily he can see when there is too much or too little or when something is damaged, deteriorating or missing. As far as possible, therefore, stock should be stored on open racks, open shelves, wire cages or stacked in the open. Good visibility is also an encouragement to tidiness – another safeguard.

Good protection is necessary in every sense of the word. Stocks must be protected against the weather, against fire, against damage and against people. Visibility should not be an invitation to anyone to walk in and walk off with material. Goods in the open should be protected with heavy-duty wire-mesh fencing. Inside buildings, it is better to have a lock-fast caged area rather than a closed room. If possible, this should be within sight of your desk or office, so that you can see who enters it, what they do there and what they take out with them.

Your stock-control system need not be elaborate. Computerized systems have no place in the small business. What you need is a simple card-index system which can be classified by alphabetical or numerical codes, according to your needs. On the card for each type of material should be entered every movement of material into or out of stock *on the day it happens*, so that by the end of the day, each card shows exactly what is there.

Each card should also show the *re-order quantity*. As entries are made, the stock balance should be compared with this and if it has dropped below this figure, the card should be marked with a coloured tab. At least once a week, you should look through the file, pick out the tabbed cards and prepare orders.

Checking the card stock against physical stock should be done much more frequently than the traditional annual stock-taking. Daily or weekly, you should take a batch of cards and check them against physical stock, making a list of any *stock differences*, whether plus or minus. At the same time, the material should be examined for damage or deterioration. Depending upon the total value of the stock in relation to your business, you should plan to cover the total stock in this way on a monthly or quarterly cycle.

CHAPTER 12

Decisions, Decisions, Decisions

The process of starting a business gives rise to many decisions, which come in all shapes and sizes. Some require careful study while others must be made in haste. Some must be made by you, some by others, while some should not be made at all. The purpose of this chapter is to show you how to discriminate between different decisions and choose the right method for making each.

Cost is an important factor in making many decisions but there are different types of cost and use of the wrong one will lead to wrong decisions. An explanation is therefore given of the main types of cost and how they may – and may not – be used in decision making.

Decision making

A popular view of the entrepreneur is a fat man with a big cigar behind a big desk, past which flows a constant stream of underlings, each stating his problem and receiving an instant decision. This caricature illustrates three errors of decision making: the enterpreneur is making too many decisions; he makes them too quickly; his staff are not learning. Perhaps there are a few super-entrepreneurs who can make the right decision intuitively and quickly but most businessmen have to do it the hard way – by thinking.

You should distinguish at the outset between *strategic* and *tactical* decisions. For instance, when starting a business, you have to decide whether to sell only for cash or to give credit. This is a basic strategic decision which affects working capital, accounting methods, stationery, staff requirements and probably sales. It will lead to many tactical

decisions, such as whether credit should be given to a particular customer and on what terms.

The strategic decision should not be made in haste; you
should study the implications in some detail before deciding. But the salesman should be able to give a tactical
decision very quickly by consulting a set of guidelines. This
illustrates another point: strategic decisions should be made
at the top; tactical decisions should be made close to 'the
action'.

Step one in making a decision is to be sure you understand what it is all about. Is the problem that you see the real
one or just a symptom of a wider or deeper problem? Remember that in a new business, when you encounter many
problems for the first time, what seems to be a unique problem may be just the first of a series.

Step two is to ask yourself, 'Do I have to decide now?' If
there is no hurry, postpone it. Beware of becoming 'decision
happy' – a disease which new businessmen sometimes catch.
Circumstances may change so why waste time making an
unnecessary decision? Even if you still have to decide later,
you may have thought of a better idea in the meantime.

Step three is to consider whether it is a strategic or a tactical decision. If the latter, how far down the line can you
push the decision? What information and guidelines need to
be provided to help those who decide? Not only is a tactical
decision likely to be better if made at the 'workface', because the staff there know more of the facts, but it gives your
staff more experience, strengthens their loyalty and saves
you time.

Step four, if it is a strategic decision, is to lay down the
ground rules for this particular problem. What are the objectives which have to be met and the side-effects which have
to be avoided? How does this problem affect your overall
business strategy? By what criteria will you measure
success? Which criteria are essential and which only desirable?

Step five is to think up possible solutions and assess the cost of each, in time and money, and its possible consequences.

Step six is to test these solutions against the criteria. Testing against the essential criteria may eliminate some. Making the final choice may be straightforward or may need methods like those used by Sally (Chapter 3) or George (Chapter 4).

Step seven is to pause and reflect before moving into action. Can you live with this decision? Have you the personality and strength of character to carry it through? What risks are involved? Is there another solution which is nearly as effective but much less risky? How are you going to implement it – who does what? Is your existing control system adequate to monitor progress or do you have to change it?

Having finally made up your mind, stop agonizing. Go ahead and do it and deviate only if there is very strong evidence that it is no longer the right decision.

Cost calculations

When studying alternative methods of doing something, cost is usually an important factor. But there are different types of cost and it is essential to use the right one for each particular application. So far in this book, when I have talked of cost I have meant *total cost*, i.e. the sum of all items of expenditure. This is the figure you need to know to calculate the overall profits of a business.

It is unusual, however, to make or sell only one article in the course of a year – most businesses deal in many articles. When considering what price to charge, you need to know the *unit cost*, i.e. the cost of making one article. Table III shows how this is worked out for a business making five hundred articles a year.

When calculating total profits, it is common to exclude your own salary since, for tax purposes, this may be lumped

Table III – Calculation of unit cost

Cost element	Total cost £ per annum	Unit cost £ each
Labour	10,000	20.00
Materials	5,000	10.00
Transport	2,000	4.00
Rent	1,500	3.00
Rates	500	1.00
Insurance	200	0.40
Professional charges	300	0.60
Interest	1,000	2.00
Depreciation	400	0.80
	20,900	41.80

together with profits. However, if you are using the figures to decide a selling price, you should add an item for your time, charged at what you would have to pay a replacement. For instance, if you value your own time at £6,000 per annum in the above example, the total cost becomes £26,900 and the unit cost £53.80 per article.

You may want to know what it will cost to make and sell just a little bit more, i.e. the *marginal cost*. This obviously does not affect all cost elements uniformly and the method of calculation is shown in Table IV.

This shows how attractive it is to increase sales by 5 per cent. The cost of the extra articles is only £16 each instead of £41.80, since only three cost elements have been affected – materials, transport and interest. These are known as *variable costs*. The other cost elements, which are unchanged, are known as *fixed costs*. A warning must be given at this point: it is dangerous to assume that you can afford to cut prices drastically to achieve extra sales – for a fuller explanation see Chapter 20.

Many businesses make and sell more than one product, which makes it more difficult to calculate the unit cost of each. Although some cost elements, the *direct costs*, may be

Table IV – Calculation of marginal cost

Cost element	Total cost		Extra cost	Marginal cost
	500 items	525 items	25 items	
	£	£	£	£ each
Labour	10,000	10,000	—	—
Materials	5,000	5,250	250	10.00
Transport	2,000	2,100	100	4.00
Rent	1,500	1,500	—	—
Rates	500	500	—	—
Insurance	200	200	—	—
Professional charges	300	300	—	—
Interest	1,000	1,050	50	2.00
Depreciation	400	400	—	—
	20,900	21,300	400	16.00

known fairly accurately, the allocation of the others, the *indirect costs* or *overheads*, is to some extent approximate and can become very time-consuming if one tries to be too precise.

It is possible to build up an elaborate system for allocating overhead costs to individual products, sometimes via other cost elements. It is quite good fun and computers can be used for the 'number-crunching' but it just isn't worth it in a small business. Indeed some of the largest and most efficient companies have abandoned such methods, so perhaps it isn't worth it for any business.

Some costing systems of the kind mentioned above purport to show, to the fifth decimal place, the precise cost of making each product. When such a cost is higher than the selling price, it is sometimes argued that the product should be discontinued. Such a decision should not be based on artificial 'product costs' but on *out-of-pocket costs*, i.e. an assessment of how much hard cash would actually be saved if you stopped making that product.

This can be illustrated by the experience of David, who has a small factory making a variety of products. His new book-keeper pointed out that Product X, of which 200 per annum were sold at a price of £15, cost £19 each to make and suggested that David should stop making it. Fortunately, David talked to his accountant before taking any action and between them they estimated the out-of-pocket costs given in Table V.

Table V – Cost of making Product X

Cost element	Total cost	Out-of-pocket cost
	£	£
Labour	1,500	—
Materials	1,000	1,000
Transport	300	50
Rent	400	—
Rates	150	—
Insurance	50	—
Interest	250	50
Depreciation	150	—
	3,800	1,100

As the table shows, all of the Materials are saved but only the petrol under Transport and only part of the Interest. There is no saving in Labour since one cannot pay off part of a man, nor is there any cash saving in Rent, Rates, Insurance or Depreciation.

If the product were discontinued, there would be a reduction of £15 × 200 = £3,000 per annum in sales income. The reduction in cost would not be £3,800 but £1,100 which would result in a net loss of £3,000 − £1,100 = £1,900 per annum. The accountant suggested that David should consider (1) increasing the selling price, (2) increasing the sales volume (since the marginal cost is less than £15), or (3) introducing a new product to replace Product X. If all of these failed, however, he advised David to continue making Product X.

Investment decisions

Before making a decision on any investment, there are three figures which you should calculate. The first is the *return on investment*, i.e. the annual profit you expect to make, expressed as a percentage of the total investment (fixed plus working capital). This shows the attractiveness of the proposal, as an investment, in comparison with what could be obtained by investing the capital in other ways.

The second figure is the *payout time*, i.e. the number of years it will take for the profits to repay the original investment. This tells you how soon you will get your money back to use in other ways. It is particularly important when you suspect the market may exist for only a limited period of time.

The third figure is the *breakeven point*, i.e. the level of production or sales at which income and expenditure exactly balance each other. This tells you how much fluctuation in turnover can be tolerated.

These can be illustrated by the case of Malcolm, who is thinking of installing a new machine costing £10,000 in his existing factory. He can find the additional working capital of £2,000 from his present resources but he will need to borrow the £10,000 fixed capital at an interest rate of 15 per cent. The machine has a capacity of 1,000 components per annum which he expects to sell at £40 each. He needs to engage two more operators to run it but the existing sales staff can handle the output. The income and expenditure at different levels of output are shown in Table VI.

His total investment is £10,000 + £2,000 = £12,000, and at full capacity his profit is £4,000, giving a *return on investment* of £4,000/£12,000 = 33⅓ per cent. The *payout time* is £12,000/£4,000 = 3.0 years.

To find the *breakeven point*, the figures for the three

Table VI – Profitability of Malcolm's new component

Output of components	500	750	1,000
Expenditure			
Labour	12,000	12,000	12,000
Materials	10,000	15,000	20,000
Interest	1,500	1,500	1,500
Depreciation (25%)	2,500	2,500	2,500
	26,000	31,000	36,000
Income	20,000	30,000	40,000
Profit/(Loss)	(6,000)	(1,000)	4,000

output levels are drawn on a graph. The breakeven point is
where the expenditure line crosses the income line which, as
Figure 1 shows, is at an annual output of 800 components,
i.e. 80 per cent of capacity. Below this he will make a loss.

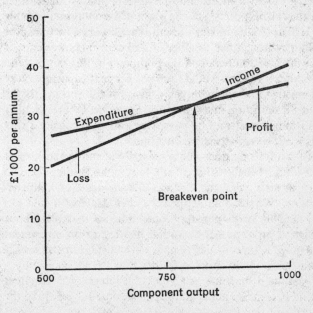

Figure 1. Breakeven Point

In making any investment decision, one is trying to judge the potential rewards in relation to the risks involved. The purpose in calculating the above figures is to quantify the rewards and risks to make it easier to assess them.

The return on investment from Malcolm's proposal ($33\frac{1}{3}$ per cent) seems reasonable in comparison, say, with the 10–12 per cent gross he could get by investing in a building society. It is also more than double the rate of interest on his borrowed money, so he makes a clear profit. The payout time (3.0 years) is also good, since he anticipates there being a long-term demand for the components. In short, the rewards seem attractive.

The risks revealed by the breakeven point are, however, considerable. To keep in profit, he is confined to the narrow range of 80–100 per cent capacity, which makes little allowance for today's uncertainties. Even if he gets a firm contract for the full output, he may be prevented from producing this by strikes at his supplier's or customer's works, by transport holdups through bad weather or strikes or by power cuts. If he were able to operate at the mid-point of this range – and most entrepreneurs would think 90 per cent capacity a very optimistic production target – his profit drops to £2,000, giving a return on investment of $16\frac{2}{3}$ per cent, barely higher than the interest rate he pays. One can only conclude that this is not a very attractive investment.

Of course one does not necessarily abandon the idea at this point, because the calculation methods allow one to play around with the figures and answer questions beginning, 'What would happen if . . .' *IF* Malcolm could run the machine with part-time operators, so that the labour cost was proportional to output, the return on investment and payout time would remain unchanged, but the breakeven point would drop to 50 per cent. *IF* he could buy a second-hand machine at £5,000, the return on investment would become 86 per cent, the payout time 1.2 years and the breakeven point 69 per cent. *IF* he could buy a different machine costing £20,000 which needed only one operator, the return on investment would become 27 per cent, the payout time 3.7 years and the breakeven point 69 per cent. The first two of these would be worth further study; if they could be combined, the scheme would become very attractive indeed – try working it out.

CHAPTER 13

Watching the Business

Running a business without controls is like driving a car in the dark without lights. From the noise of the engine, you have a rough idea of the speed. An occasional glimpse of the instruments in the lights of a passing vehicle tells you how well the car is performing. If you know the road well and there is a bit of moonlight, you may get there eventually but it is a slow process and rather stressful.

How different is the same journey with lights. You can see the dangers ahead and take avoiding action. You can see when to turn in a new direction. Above all, you are in full control of the vehicle and can use its power efficiently and to its full capacity.

The same applies when you run a business with well-designed controls. Not only can you make more effective use of the resources available but you get timely warning of coming hazards. Moreover, you have the reassurance of knowing when you are on course and can stop worrying. The purpose of this chapter is to show you how to design and use controls for *your* business.

Business controls

When starting a business for the first time, there is so much to learn. One learns by (1) observing closely what is happening, (2) comparing this with what one wants to happen, (3) deducing the reason for any difference, and (4) making changes to bring the business back on course. This continuous cycle of observation, comparison, deduction and correction is carried out systematically by means of *business controls*.

There can be too few controls, so that the boss does not know what is going on. There can also be too many controls, as anyone will testify who has worked in a place with a computer-happy management accountant. A sense of proportion is needed to get the total effort right.

In a new business, you should err at first on the side of too few rather than too many controls. It is easy to add more controls later, as the need arises. It is more difficult to detect and abolish unnecessary controls, once they have become established.

Some businesses rely mainly upon financial controls. In many cases the conversion of direct observations into money terms simply causes delay and creates more paperwork. In addition, financial figures are frequently regarded as confidential and reported only to the boss who, in turn, has to look at them and tell someone what to do. This someone is often the person who took the original observation and is quite capable of reaching the same conclusion as the boss. This roundabout method causes still further delay and the employee is made to feel that it is not his responsibility.

These problems can largely be avoided by using *direct controls*, as far as possible, instead of *indirect controls*. For example, in running a fleet of vehicles, petrol consumption is an important cost element. This can be measured directly in terms of miles per gallon and used in this form as a control. Converting this to pence per mile simply creates extra book-keeping work and causes delay. Moreover, when petrol prices are fluctuating, it is not immediately obvious whether a change in fuel costs is due to fuel consumption or fuel price.

Different controls need to be studied at different frequencies and it is a mistake to try to apply the same frequency to all. For instance, if you have a shop, you will probably want to know your takings daily, your wage bill weekly and your stock level monthly.

After you have been running for, say, three months, have

a critical look at your whole control system. Look at those you have been using to see whether any can be cut out or reduced in frequency. Look also to see whether any can be simplified. Look back over the previous three months' happenings and consider whether any of your crises could be avoided in future by setting up new controls or increasing the frequency of existing ones.

Yardsticks

As mentioned above, observing (or counting or measuring or calculating) something is but the first step in a control. The figure obtained must then be compared with a *yardstick* to check whether or not it is satisfactory. There are three types of yardstick – theoretical, historical and comparative.

Theoretical yardsticks are obtained by calculation or from makers' figures. For instance, one can calculate how much product should be made from a given quantity of raw material or how many hours per week a machine is available for use. One can use manufacturer's figures for fuel or power consumption.

Historical yardsticks are, in essence, how it was done last month or last year. One of the purposes of control systems is to provide information of this sort, so that yardsticks can be updated regularly.

Comparative yardsticks are based on how other businesses perform. Information for deriving these can be obtained from trade magazines, textbooks, suppliers, trade associations, etc. One of the reasons for studying these is to counteract smugness. You may think you are doing well compared with last year, but last year you may have done poorly by normal trade standards.

Instead of comparing the observed figure with three different yardsticks, it is common to use a single *target* which takes into account all three yardsticks. Different targets can be set for different days of the week or different times of the year to allow for daily or seasonal fluctuations in the pattern of trade. Such adjustments make the target more realistic and the control more useful.

When starting a new business, one often has little option but to use a target. The theoretical yardstick may be quite unrealistic in the early days, the historical yardstick is not yet established and you may not have found enough information to build a comparative yardstick.

Your first target may be based on the assumptions you have made when planning the business. These can be modified in the light of experience, a process which is helped strongly by the very existence of the control.

Presentation of controls

Whereas a 'record' is written down and may never be looked at again, a 'control' is intended to be looked at and used to make a conscious decision. A control should therefore be designed so as to make it easy to look at and decide what, if anything, to do. In other words, the effectiveness of a control is influenced by the way it is presented.

Controls may be presented in a variety of forms. They may be on a handwritten chit, pre-printed form, typed statement, computer printout or some other form of 'numbers on paper'. Alternatively, they may be drawn on a graph, bar chart or some other pictorial form. The choice of numerical or pictorial display depends partly on the information presented and partly on the work involved in presentation – but mainly upon the preferences of the recipient. If you are very numerate you will probably prefer to see 'the figures'. If you are less numerate, you may get a better feeling for trends from 'pictures'.

Whichever method is employed, it is preferable for the *target* to be shown on the same piece of paper or chart for quick reference. One should be able to see, at a glance, whether or not the activity is 'on target' within the agreed range. One also wants to be able to see, from the same presentation, how big the deviation is. Controls sometimes show not only the actual figure but also the amount this is off target – accountants call this the *variance*. This may be expressed in units or as a percentage of the target figure.

Fluctuations are often encountered from one reading to the next. This may be a genuine fluctuation in the reading or it may be due to approximations made for the sake of speedy reporting. (A basic principle of controls is that it is better to get an approximate figure quickly than a precise figure slowly.) These fluctuations are often 'smoothed' by presenting the figures cumulatively or as a moving average.

When presenting controls in graphical or pictorial form, care must be taken in choosing the scale. Not only must it cover the whole range of readings likely to be encountered, but a deviation which is significant should *look* significant. Similarly, a minor fluctuation should not look like a major deviation.

The size of the piece of paper is usually unimportant in relation to the significance of the results. It can be important, however, for ease of filing for future use. In Chapter 7, it was mentioned that one of the six 'thinkbooks' was for controls. It is therefore convenient if all the controls which you wish to keep in this book, whether numerical or graphical, are produced on the appropriate size of paper.

Wall charts are a convenient method of presentation when the information should be readily available to a number of people. During the early days of the business, however, you may not wish that everyone who visits your workplace should have instant access to, for example, your production or sales statistics. Wall charts can be obtained with lockable doors or roller blinds, but it may be safer not to use wall charts for any information which you want to keep confidential.

Use of controls

The way in which controls can be used is best illustrated by examples. Alex runs a small production engineering shop with two assistants. Figure 2 shows the *monthly production control* he has painted on the wall of his shop. He marks up the graph daily with a felt pen, then wipes it off at the end of the month and starts again.

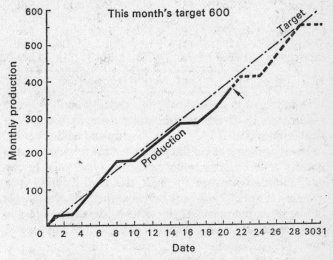

Figure 2.   Monthly Production Control

This month's target is high and it is a 5-weekend month but, as the graph shows, he was doing all right until the 10th when Alf, one of his assistants, fell ill. Alf returned on the 20th but the damage had been done. As the dotted line shows, even at normal full production until the month end, Alex is not going to make it. So he decides to work overtime during the weekend 23rd/24th.

Dorothy has a small grocery store. Unlike Alex, who uses the calendar month, she works on a year of thirteen 4-week months for control purposes. Table VII shows the *weekly takings control* she keeps in her thinkbook and shows only to her accountant.

Table VII – Weekly takings control: Month 6

	Target	Actual takings – week number				Total
		21	22	23	24	
	£	£	£	£	£	£
Monday	100	82	—	109	93	284
Tuesday	150	163	143	167	139	612
Wednesday	80	96	87	72	67	322
Thursday	170	182	172	164	168	686
Friday	200	211	195	202	204	812
Saturday	300	365	283	314	310	1,272
Total	1,000	1,099	880	1,028	981	3,988

Dorothy put in the end column, headed 'Total', to check her arithmetic. If she gets the same figure in the bottom right-hand corner (£3,988) by adding up and adding across, she feels confident of her figures. The astute reader will have noted that Wednesday is early closing day and that Friday and Saturday account for half the total takings. The Monday in week 22 is a bank holiday, which hits the takings in that week, but this is largely offset by the extra takings in the previous week, as customers stock up for the long week-end.

Donald runs a taxi business, in which one of the main costs is petrol. To keep an eye on vehicle efficiency (and to discourage theft) he uses a *petrol consumption control*. Each morning he tops up the petrol tank, adds this quantity to any put in during the previous twenty-four hours and takes the speedometer reading. The effect of daily fluctuations in run length and in the level in the petrol tank is reduced by using a 7-day moving average, i.e. he divides the mileage for the last seven days by the gallons consumed in the same period to give the average miles per gallon over the last seven days. This is illustrated in Table VIII.

Table VIII – Daily petrol consumption: W/E 25/2/79

| Day | Speedo reading | Day | | | 7-day ave. mpg |
		miles	gallons	mpg	
Monday	23,124	237	8.9	26.7	26.9
Tuesday	23,448	324	12.0	27.0	26.9
Wednesday	23,863	415	15.4	26.9	27.0
Thursday	24,212	349	12.9	27.1	27.0
Friday	24,662	450	16.7	26.9	27.1
Saturday	25,233	571	20.9	27.3	27.1
Sunday	25,489	256	9.6	26.7	27.0

Review of controls

To guard against the 'controls' degenerating into 'records',
it is a valuable discipline to make a regular *monthly review*,
as I do in my own business. Once a month I study each
control in turn, comparing the actual results against target,
noting those which are 'on target' and trying to account for
the deviations in the others.

I write down brief comments on each, particularly when
action is required, and part of the review is concerned with
checking whether I have taken the actions decided in previous months and how it has worked out.

Occasionally I decide to change the target, either because
it was badly set in the first place or because circumstances
have changed. One must be careful, however, not to use this
as an excuse for not taking corrective action. I complete
each review by making a *cash-flow forecast* for the next
month, mainly to see whether there is some spare cash which
can be put into the savings account or whether it will be
necessary to withdraw from the savings account.

At the end of each financial year, I make an *annual
review*. In addition to studying the profit outturn, I re-examine my business objectives and business strategy to see if any
modification is needed. Then I study each control in turn,

asking myself the following questions: (1) what is this designed to control? (2) is it still needed? (3) is it effective? (4) can it be simplified? Over the past five years, I have been able to reduce the number of controls from nine to six and some of these have been simplified.

CHAPTER 14

Watching the Money

Time is divided into three phases – Past, Present and Future. Corresponding to each is a different financial technique. Your *accounts* are a record of the *past*. You cannot change the past but you can learn from it how to do better in future, so your accounts should be kept in a way which makes this easy. Your *cash flow* dictates what you can do in the *present*. If you have not got the cash to pay the bills which are now due, you are in trouble, so the object of controlling cash flow is to ensure that money is available when you need it. Your *budgets* represent what you intend to do in the *future*. They enable you to plan what to do and, in particular, when to do it.

There is a constant flow as time progresses: yesterday's budget becomes today's cash flow and then tomorrow's accounts. The purpose of this chapter is to discuss these three financial techniques and other means by which you can 'watch the money' in *your* business.

Accounts

Let me distinguish here between 'keeping records' and 'keeping accounts'. Some of my accountant friends tell horror stories of arriving at a small business to prepare their accounts for the first time and being handed a cardboard box or bulldog clip full of tatty invoices and receipts.

If the collection is complete, the accountant can prepare a set of accounts and tell the owner – for the first time – how much profit or loss he is making. Frequently the collection is not complete and a long wrangle ensues with the tax inspector, a wrangle which can be expensive for the owner in terms of accountant's fees and missed opportunities for tax saving.

I am sure you will agree that this is not the way to run a *successful* business. Not only does this incur expense which could be avoided, but the owner is not using the information to guide the conduct of his business. He doesn't know which are the profitable parts of the business to be expanded nor where there are losses to be cut. Such an entrepreneur may be keeping records – but he is not keeping accounts.

Records must be kept to satisfy tax and other legal requirements but from these records certain figures should be extracted to enable you to see – as you go along – how the business is progressing. Accounts provide an up-to-date picture of what is buried in the records, so that you do not have to dig through the latter every time you want information.

Keeping accounts is, of course, an unprofitable exercise in the sense that no customer is paying you for doing so. The effort devoted to this should therefore be kept to a minimum. Nevertheless, you will find it profitable to keep a certain number of accounts, not only to calculate profit and loss for tax purposes but to enable you to run the business more efficiently.

Particular trades have particular needs but there are certain accounts which most businesses should keep. You need capital expenditure accounts, so that you can calculate how much 'capital allowances' can be deducted from profits before working out your tax bill.

You need operating expenditure accounts, distinguishing between goods purchased for stock and other forms of expenditure. If you obtain supplies on credit, you may need separate accounts for each creditor to ensure that bills are paid when due – but only paid once.

On the income side, you need separate accounts for cash and credit sales. In the latter case, you probably need a separate account for each customer to keep track of those who have paid their bills and those who have not – and to show when payment is overdue.

If you are registered for VAT (see Chapter 19), you need accounts to enable you to make your quarterly VAT returns. If you employ any staff, you need an account for each employee to show wages due, payments made and deductions for Pay As You Earn (PAYE) and National Health Insurance (NHI) contributions.

The above is only the bare outline of what you are likely to need; you must discuss the details with your accountant. Much of this book-keeping can be simplified by the use of pre-printed stationery and account books. Find out what is available by writing to a specialist supplier (e.g. Kalamazoo Ltd, Northfield, Birmingham B31 2RW), visiting a 'business efficiency' exhibition, looking at the stock of a large commercial stationer – or a combination of these. You must decide on your accounting system at an early stage because, although it should be easy to open or close individual accounts, it may be difficult to change the system later on.

Cash flow

The method of making a 12-month cash-flow forecast is described in Chapter 7; the same method can be used on a shorter time scale. If your cash balance is changing every day, you probably need a day-by-day forecast covering the next week. If it changes more slowly, a week-by-week forecast for the next month may be sufficient. Most of the information will come from your accounts but the budget should also be consulted to provide early warning of forthcoming major items.

Some of Britain's biggest companies have elaborate systems for collecting in surplus cash *daily* from branches all over the country and investing the total on the overnight money market. If cash control is a useful source of extra profit for established companies, it is a vital necessity for a new and struggling business.

Most people who have successfully started a business will

admit to times when the future of the business was balanced on a knife edge. They will tell (afterwards) of having to wait until a customer's cheque came in and was 'expressed' through the bank before a cheque could be cashed for wages. They were the smart ones who knew what their balance was. The less astute ones suffered the embarrassment of cheques bouncing.

The first essential in cash control lies in knowing what your bank balance is today and what it is likely to be for the next few days ahead. This is achieved by a regular cash-flow forecast, checking with the bank if necessary to ensure that your calculation of today's balance agrees with their books. In this way, you avoid issuing a cheque on Wednesday if it means you won't have enough for the wages cheque on Friday. It also means you know when cheques can be cleared normally and when they have to be 'expressed'.

The second essential is to have a consistent credit policy and apply it rigidly. Most of us hate chasing someone to pay a debt but you must learn to overcome your reluctance. As soon as a bill is overdue, start chasing – politely but firmly – and don't be too proud to go along to collect it in person rather than risk its being delayed in the post. There are methods of easing cash-flow problems, such as *factoring* or *invoice discounting*, whereby one receives an immediate advance of up to 80 per cent of the value of invoices. There is, however, usually a minimum turnover of £50,000–£100,000 and this is not the cheapest form of finance.

The third essential is to keep a tight control over cash going out. To build up a good reputation, make sure you pay bills when due – but not before. Don't pay invoices as soon as you receive them; make a note in your diary when they are due and pay them then. In many trades it is customary to offer a discount for prompt payment. If you can get $2\frac{1}{2}$ per cent off for payment within fourteen days, this is a good rate of interest but you should not do this if it means being late in paying someone else. Your cash-flow forecast will tell you when to do this and when not; obviously you should try to control your cash so that you can always take advantage of such opportunities.

One of the outward cash flows is what you pay yourself for living expenses – your *drawings*. In the early days, you should be as mean as you dare with your family and yourself. You should apply the same strict cash control to personal expenditure as you do to your business.

Budgets

In Chapter 4, I explained how to make domestic and business budgets. Once started, you should continue to make a *domestic budget* as a means of controlling cash flow out of the business. The budget deficit each month can then be picked up in your business budget, as a forecast of the drawings for that month. If you have a surplus on your domestic budget after you start your business, this provides a source of funds for expansion.

Once the business is running, you will need two separate budgets – operating and capital. The *operating budget* shows the anticipated income from the business and the day-to-day expenses of running it. The *capital budget* shows the anticipated expenditure on capital investment, e.g. equipment, vehicles, furniture, etc. and renewals of existing capital items.

Broadly speaking, items which have an expected life of more than a year are regarded as capital, but some common sense is used in interpreting the rules. For instance, if you buy a new spanner for a few pounds, this is usually classed as an operating expense, even though it is expected to last a few years. Your accountant will guide you on this rather complicated subject.

In most new businesses, the type of operating budget needed is what accountants call a *rolling annual budget*, *updated quarterly.* This means that you make a forecast of income and expenditure for twelve months ahead. Then after three months, you make a new forecast for twelve months ahead, by updating the nine months remaining of the original budget and adding on three new months. Thus your current budget is never more than three months old and it always shows the way ahead for at least nine months.

In the beginning, you will group your operating expenditure under headings such as those given in Chapter 4. Keep your budget system as simple as possible, since you will have to do most of the work – and you have other things to do. It is, however, well worth while keeping all your working papers neatly filed. This will save you a lot of time when you come to the quarterly updating. It will also enable you to answer most of the questions which are likely to arise.

The purpose of the capital budget is to collect together those capital items which you hope to implement, so that you can get a comprehensive picture of future commitments. These will probably be few in the beginning, but it is worth while adopting some system for dealing with them.

List each item, in sequence, under the following three headings: (1) *Essential* (to meet legal or other unavoidable requirements); (2) *Profitable* (ranked in order of attractiveness, as assessed by the methods described in Chapter 12); (3) *Desirable* (a very low priority indeed).

Against each item, you should list the expenditure, month by month, during the next year. Then total the monthly expenditure and refer to your operating budget, the source of internal capital. If this is inadequate, can you – and are you willing to – borrow the money? You may want to rephase expenditure or delete some items until you achieve a budget which is realistic.

Taxation

The basis on which tax is assessed for a new business can be
illustrated by the case of Phyllis, who started a toy-making
business as a sole trader on 1 July 1976.

For the tax year 1976/77, she was assessed on the profits
she made during this tax year, which was her first nine
months of business. In practice, the tax inspector usually
waits until the accounts are available for the first complete
year of business and assesses tax on a proportionate basis.
This keeps it simple and, in her case, he assessed her business
income at nine-twelfths of her profit for Year 1
(1.7.76–30.6.77), i.e. 9/12 of £6,000 = £4,500.

During the first few months, however, Phyllis spent a lot
on materials and was very busy making toys to build up a
stock but sold very few. She had kept a record of her
monthly income and expenditure, from which she was able
to calculate that her profits during the period 1.7.76–31.3.77
was, in fact, only £2,700. She submitted these figures to the
tax inspector, who accepted them without demur. In short,
by challenging the first assessment, and having the figures to
support her case, she reduced her taxable business income
from £4,500 to £2,700, resulting in a tax saving of about
£600.

For tax year 1977/78, the tax inspector assessed her on
the profits for the first year of business (1.7.76–30.6.77),
i.e. £6,000.

For tax year 1978/79, the tax inspector *again* assessed her
on the profits for the first year of business (1.7.76–30.6.77),
i.e. £6,000. This is because the 'Income from Trade, Pro-
fession or Vocation' is taxed under Schedule D, which assesses tax on the income during the 'business year' which
ends during the twelve months preceding the tax year. The
twelve months preceding tax year 1978/79 ran from 6.4.77
to 5.4.78. The business year which ended during this period
was the one ending on 30.6.77, i.e. Phyllis's first business

year. All of the above complications are simply the way in which the tax inspector gets a new business on to that basis. From now on, Phyllis will be assessed on a regular basis in arrears, i.e. Year 2 for tax year 1979/80 and so on.

The above example illustrates a very simple case. You should talk to your accountant about how you are likely to be affected. Phyllis also shows how a bit of attention to your tax affairs can pay off. Of course the object of running a business is not to pay the minimum tax, since you can easily pay no tax at all by making no profit. The object of running a business is to make the maximum after-tax profit.

The profit on which you are assessed is rarely exactly the same as that which you work out from your income and expenditure. This is not because you keep two sets of books – one for the owner and one for tax – a practice which is ascribed to some countries. It is because the inspector may not accept some expenditure which you think should be charged to the business, such as reference books, entertaining UK customers or your own meals when travelling on business. The usual practice is to keep your books in a prudent fashion and then correct your profit figure for the items the inspector disallows.

Security

No chapter on 'watching the money' would be complete without some reference to security, i.e. avoiding financial loss through accident, damage or theft. One obvious method of avoiding loss is to insure against it, so that you get compensation if it happens. You should therefore take out adequate insurance cover on your *property* – buildings and contents, vehicles and equipment used outside your premises. I emphasize the word 'adequate' since, if you insure for less than the real value, the insurance company is likely to pay only a proportion of your loss.

If you employ staff, you need *employer's liability* insurance and it may be prudent to insure against *theft* or *embezzlement*. It is also wise to insure against *accidental damage* to third parties on your premises or by action of your employees or yourself elsewhere. If appropriate, you may need *professional indemnity* insurance in case of customers claiming against poor services provided by your staff or yourself. You may also wish to take *loss of earnings* insurance in case your business is closed down for a time by fire or other damage.

It is much better, of course, if you can prevent any of these things happening and, indeed, insurance companies may refuse to pay out if you do not take reasonable precautions. Hence you need good fastenings on windows and doors and premises should not be left unlocked when unattended. If there is a fire risk in your business, you may need to fit fire extinguishers and pay particular attention to working methods and storage of inflammable materials. Some protection against third-party claims can be ensured by careful wording of contracts and good staff training.

It is unpleasant to think about your own staff cheating you but one must face up to facts. Some people are dishonest and others who are usually honest may be tempted by an easy opportunity. The best protection is to make it difficult for someone to steal from you, by using good equipment (e.g. cash register, safe) and good business systems. Nor is it only cash you must guard – goods can be smuggled out or sold to accomplices at low prices.

The best safeguard is your own behaviour. If you show that you care about protecting your property and are determined that your staff care too, they will respond. If you refuse to tolerate sloppy book-keeping or cash-handling, your staff will respect you. If you allow staff a discount on goods for personal use, they are less likely to steal. If you prosecute shop-lifters, your staff will know you are serious. In short, if you devote time, money and effort to protecting your business, the individual looking for an easy mark will go elsewhere and the honest employee will be encouraged to support you.

While many security precautions are simply common sense, expertise is sometimes required. Advice can be obtained from many quarters, e.g. police, fire service, insurance companies, equipment and system suppliers, trade associations, etc. Much of this advice is free but not all is disinterested. Don't forget also your 'three wise men' – bank manager, solicitor and accountant. Most of the above points seem obvious but they are sometimes overlooked by the new entrepreneur with many other things on his mind. If you take a risk, let it be a deliberate one – not from thoughtlessness.

CHAPTER 15
Watching the Clock

Time is a unique commodity – it cannot be directly bought, sold, leased, borrowed or stored. Because your own time is often the limitation on business growth, you have every reason to use your time effectively. And yet, at the end of each day, when you look at the list of jobs you had hoped to complete, I'll bet that many are still not crossed off.

To some extent you are still learning how long it takes to do things, but this is not the whole story. You are beginning to realize that, as an entrepreneur, you must use your time much more effectively than you did as an employee. You need to learn new techniques to break the 'time barrier'. The purpose of this chapter is to show you how.

Where time flies

You may think you know how you spend your time at present. This is probably untrue but don't take my word for it. Try this little experiment. Write down on a piece of paper the activities on which you believe you spend most of your time; add a further item for 'other activities'. Put against each the percentage of your time that you spend on that activity and put the paper in a drawer.

Now keep a detailed record for a week using a technique called *activity sampling*. Take a sheet of paper for each day, mark the time at quarter-hour intervals down the left-hand side, and rule a column for each of your selected activities, plus an extra one for 'other activities'. Each quarter of an hour put a tick under the heading for what you are doing at that moment. At the end of each day, count the number of ticks under each heading then total them for the week and calculate each as a percentage of the total.

If the result of this experiment agrees with your estimate, then you are one of those rare individuals who really does know how he spends his time. You are more likely to be surprised and perhaps disappointed. Indeed you may need a second run with a different set of headings to break down the large percentage under 'other activities'. This experiment will have taught you a little about your present time usage and perhaps convinced you that you could improve upon it.

It is tempting to wonder if there is an 'ideal' time distribution which, if adopted, would ensure the most effective use of your time. When one thinks of it, however, a 'norm' which could apply to everyone is just not possible. Consider how different the work pattern is in, for example: shopkeeping, running a typing bureau, jobbing engineering, home toymaking, snackbar operation. Nevertheless, for a given individual in a particular business there is an optimum pattern but it has to be found by study of your own time usage.

You are probably familiar with the distinction between *tax avoidance* and *tax evasion*. In the former, you try to arrange your affairs so as to minimize the amount of tax due; in the latter, you do not pay the tax which is due. The former is legal, the latter illegal. One of the most effective ways of saving time is to practise *work avoidance*, i.e. minimize the amount of work which needs to be done.

Your first reaction might be to protest that only a fool would do work which needn't be done. I make no comment – just look again at your experimental time record. Can you say, hand on heart, that every job was absolutely essential? Why did it have to be done? Why that way? Why then? How many jobs were done because you had got into a habit or because you enjoyed doing them? Can you honestly say that there is no scope for skilful pruning?

Passing it on

The next best thing to avoiding a job is to pass it on to an
assistant whose time is, presumably, less valuable than yours
– in short, to *delegate*. This is a popular word in all the
management textbooks and everyone is in favour of delegation – in theory. Nevertheless, if you look around, you
see that many people do not delegate – in practice – so let us
look at some of the obstacles to delegation.

Delegation exposes the boss to *risk*. The assistant may not
assess the situation correctly, may not decide on the correct
measures to be taken and may not carry enough weight to
get cooperation from others. Another obstacle is *fear*. The
assistant may become so good at the job that he gets a better
job with your competitor or even starts his own business in
competition. Yet a third obstacle is *perfectionism*. It is hard
to decide, in cold blood, to allow a job to be done by someone who, in your opinion, is less competent than yourself.

From my own experience, I learned how to delegate only
when I had a project which involved so much work against
tight deadlines that I *had* to delegate or the job would not
have been done on time. The choice before me was not between delegating and not delegating but simply which tasks
should be delegated. The ones I did not delegate kept me so
busy that I had no time to breathe down the necks of my
assistants.

This experience did my assistants a power of good. None
were broken by it, some increased noticeably in stature and
all learned how to handle jobs which they might otherwise
have waited years to learn.

For my part, I learned that if one has the courage to overcome the obstacles and try delegation, there are very real
rewards. I emerged from the project with considerable credit
as a result of the efforts of my assistants. I also learned that
the way to make delegation work lies in the three Ts – *think,
train, trust.*

THINK carefully about which tasks you should delegate. Generally speaking, these are ones which do not demand your personal presence, which are not closely interwoven with your other tasks, with which you need not be continuously au fait and which your assistant can do well enough.

TRAIN your assistants·in how to do the job properly. The quicker they learn to do it, the sooner you are released to concentrate on the jobs which cannot be delegated.

TRUST your assistant to do the job once he has been trained. Don't hover around all the time but check sufficiently often to reassure yourself – and him – that he is doing it properly. Support your assistant when something goes wrong and show others that he is acting on your behalf with the full weight of your authority behind him. The post-mortem can be done afterwards – in private.

One can, of course, delegate too much as well as too little, but this is rare. The real danger to guard against is allowing delegation to become abdication, i.e. the renunciation of responsibility. Talk over the job with your assistant from time to time. Share your thoughts and thus give him a better chance of predicting how you would behave when something new crops us. The key to effective delegation is to give your assistants as much responsibility as they can take and back them all the way – but remember that the ultimate responsibility is always yours.

Ten tips for time-saving

Having reduced your workload by 'avoiding' some tasks and delegating others, you are left with the balance which you still have to do yourself. Here are ten different ways in

which time can be saved. See how many you can apply to
your business.

(1) *Business or 'busyness'* – Do you really want to work
more efficiently or are you secretly afraid that this might
result in your sitting, twiddling your thumbs? The success of
your business depends upon results – not efforts. If you can
achieve the same results with less effort, the time saved can
be used to produce still more results – and still more profit.
Don't confuse business with 'busyness'.

(2) *Working methods* – When a task first arises, one often
has to improvise a method quickly to get the job done. This
method soon becomes habitual, because it is easier to copy
how it was done last time than work out how to do it better.
Step back, from time to time, and examine your own working methods as critically as those of your assistants.

(3) *Job sequence* – Jobs differ in their demands upon us.
Some require more physical exertion than others; some need
much mental effort. Such jobs take less time to do early in
the day, before you are tired. Other jobs are relatively un-
taxing and can be done at the end of the day. Try to make
your job sequence fit your fatigue curve.

(4) *Fragmentation* – If you never seem to have 'time to
think', it may be a sign that your day suffers from what is
called 'fragmentation', i.e. it is broken up into too many
little bits. Try to set aside an hour at a fixed time each day
and train your staff to protect you from interruptions during
this time. Use this time for jobs which need a period of
continuous concentration. Going to work an hour early is
often an effective way of solving this problem.

(5) *Grasshopper mind* – For many businesses you need to
acquire a 'grasshopper mind', i.e. the ability to switch
rapidly and frequently from one subject to another. In some
people this becomes a habit or a means of escape. When

they encounter a difficult part of a task, they lay it aside 'until they have more time'. But problems do not usually solve themselves lying in a pending basket and it takes time to pick up the threads again when the task is resumed. If you suspect you may suffer from this fault, keep a record for a few days of every time you change subject and note honestly whether it was due to interruption (fragmentation) or self-inflicted (grasshopper mind).

(6) *Travel* – If you do a lot of travelling, it might be worth keeping a log for a few weeks to see how much time is spent this way. Analyse each trip and ask yourself if: (a) it was really necessary, and (b) you used the most time-effective transport. Travel can become a habit or even an escape, conscious or unconscious, from boredom or stress. Was this the real reason for any trips? It is rarely possible to do any work when driving but some kinds of work (e.g. reading, writing, thinking) can be done on the train. The latter may be more effective in using time, even if it takes longer. Or it might be worth using a driver if it allows you to work in the car.

(7) *Verbosity* – This is a common failing which is not only annoying, when practised by other people, but wastes a lot of time. Try the following methods of self-improvement. (a) Get out the correspondence file periodically and go over letters you wrote a few months ago to see how you can cut them down. (b) Before starting a meeting, discussion or telephone call jot down the main points you want to make. Check afterwards if you kept to it. (c) Force your assistants to 'keep it short' when writing or talking to you. This saves your time and obliges you to set a good example. (d) Observe how some people are able to cut others short without giving offence – and copy their technique. (e) Finally, think before you speak or write.

(8) *Thinking ahead* – Many problems can be avoided or at

least lessened, by thinking ahead. Lack of planning may cause confusion, frequent changes of instruction and duplication of effort, all of which are great time-wasters. Time for thinking doesn't just happen – it has to be made by the methods described in this chapter.

(9) *Priorities and posteriorities* – There are always more tasks to be done than you have time to do. This is usually handled by deciding on priorities. Few pay any attention to what Peter Drucker, the well-known business writer, calls 'posteriorities', i.e. the tasks you decide not to do at all. It takes courage to decide to ignore something, but why carry an item for weeks at the bottom of the list before scrapping it? You can save time by deciding at the start not to put something on the list.

(10) *Regular monitoring* – Starting a time-saving campaign is not enough – you have to keep it up. This means regular monitoring but the method used must be simple or it defeats the purpose. For five years I have kept a daily log, noting the time I switch from one job to another and allowing for significant interruptions such as long telephone calls. Each morning I summarize for the previous day the number of (quarter-hour) units spent on each task. At the month-end, the daily records are totalled to provide the basis of invoices to clients. These totals are also checked against my work plans. The whole system takes five minutes each day and an hour at the month-end. The time saving has been much greater and it has resulted in a greatly improved accuracy in planning. Moreover, I remain continuously aware of the value of time and the need to control it.

Means and ends

There are some hazards if one carries time-saving to excess. You may use a lift instead of the stairs or use the car for a journey you could walk in five minutes. The success of your business depends upon your keeping healthy, which requires exercise. If your pattern of life and work does not automatically provide exercise, you have to arrange it. If this can be combined with doing something else (e.g. moving from A to B) this is an economy, not a waste of time.

Another hazard is that you reduce contact with people too far. You should be on your guard against becoming inaccessible to assistants, customers and outside contacts. Otherwise, you will gradually cease to be kept informed about what is going on and your influence on other people will dwindle. Too much reliance on written information can be dangerous, since one misses the nuances of facial expression and voice inflection. One also loses the type of information which others are unwilling to put on paper. Moreover, although you may save a few minutes by reading instead of listening, it may take someone else much longer to write than to phone you or pop into your office. So they won't do it.

Finally, you may be tempted to skip the daily 'walk round the shop'. The Dutch have a very good proverb that 'The grass grows greener under the eye of the farmer'. During your morning tour you spot equipment that is broken or missing, dirty work places, the job someone has brought in to do in working hours, lateness or absence of staff. Employees will chat to you at their own workbench in a way they never would in your office. Thus you keep in touch with the personal affairs of each individual and morale in general. One of the great strengths of a small business is the easy access employees have to the boss. Don't throw away such an important advantage.

In short, there are dangers in time-saving if you lose your sense of proportion. Time-saving is a means to greater efficiency – not an end in itself.

CHAPTER 16

What about the Workers?

It is almost impossible to create a successful business without employing staff. This applies even to the top earners – the QC has his managing clerk, the Harley Street specialist his receptionist, the best-selling writer his agent and the pop-star his manager. In all these cases, the 'virtuoso' has engaged someone else to do part of the work, so that he can spend more time on the activity that brings in the money.

Consequently, if you are optimistic about your venture, you must accept that one day you will begin to employ other people. You may have some experience of managing others, from former jobs, but most new entrepreneurs have never carried out, from a cold start, the full process of employing staff. Where do you get them? How do you tell the good ones from the bad ones? What should you pay them? How do you get them to do what you want done?

This chapter tells you something about dealing with 'the workers'. You can also teach yourself a lot by keeping your eyes and ears open as you look at other businesses. Observe how they treat staff and the results they get. Learn from their successes – and their failures.

What staff do you need?

Think carefully about what you want your new staff to do. Do you want someone to take over part of your work or do you want a recruit with skills you lack, to widen the range of work the business can tackle? These thoughts tell you what skills the new recruit should have under 'normal' conditions. But you will encounter a lot of 'abnormal' conditions, since feast or famine is the way of life in most new businesses.

How will you use the new employee when things are slack or very busy? Odd jobs, repairs to buildings and equipment, driving the van, answering the phone, packing parcels? This adds further to the list of skills required.

Do you want someone who will do what you tell him, but no more? Or do you want someone with a bit of initiative, who can cope with the unexpected in your absence and suggest improvements in work methods? The answers to these questions will tell you the kind of personality to look for when interviewing applicants and the kind of experience to look for in their work records.

You must decide whether you want the recruit full-time or part-time. A full-time assistant provides someone available all day, who can 'mind the shop' in your absence, but you might have difficulty in using him profitably all the time. Hiring part-time staff provides greater flexibility in adjusting to workload and gives you the chance to employ a wider range of skills. In addition part-time workers such as pensioners and housewives are often easier to find and offer better value for money.

What do you pay?

In deciding what pay to offer a new recruit, there are three main considerations: (a) what you are paying existing staff, if you have any; (b) what the recruit is earning now; (c) the 'going rate' in the district for that type of work. The first figure you know; the second will vary from one applicant to another and is unknown until each applies. The third can be found from various sources: the local Jobcentre, Chamber of Trade, vacancies advertised in the local press, local employers, etc. You should collect figures from as many sources as possible and study the range.

The word 'pay' can mean several things, e.g. basic rate of pay, 'take home' pay, etc. For your purpose, the most useful meaning is probably the average gross earnings, i.e. basic pay plus overtime, bonus, commission, etc. but before

PAYE, NHI and other deductions. Check whether the pay figures you have collected are comparable and adjust them if necessary.

As a first stab at formulating a pay 'package', take what seems a good basic *pay* rate and add to this any *bonus*, *commission* and *allowances* you intend to offer. Then estimate the average hours of *overtime* and add on the appropriate payment. Take this as the minimum gross earnings and add 10 per cent to give a maximum. This represents the range of pay package you might offer, the minimum to someone just satisfactory and the maximum to a really good candidate.

How does your range fit in with the spread of figures you have collected? Compare the job you are offering with those of other local employers, taking into account the conditions of employment discussed below. Your range should preferably fall in the upper part of the spread because, as a new and rather insecure employer, you must expect to pay a premium to get good-quality staff. If it doesn't look right, try adjusting the basic rate, overtime and the other elements of the pay package until you get a range that does look right in comparison with the existing pay pattern.

Conditions of employment

If you hire through a Jobcentre or commercial agency, they will want to know something about working conditions to help them choose suitable applicants. If you decide to advertise, you need to mention some of the conditions in your advertisement. When you interview applicants, they will ask questions which you must answer before they will consider seriously any offer you might make. Finally, you will want to know, from your side, what extra costs you are committing yourself to before you engage someone. Therefore think carefully about *conditions of employment* before you even begin the process of hiring someone.

You are also under some legal obligations as an employer.

The Contracts of Employment Act 1972 lays down that all employees working sixteen or more hours per week must be given, not later than thirteen weeks after they start work, a written statement or contract of employment. This statement or contract must include details of

- the rate of pay and whether it is calculated on an hourly, weekly or monthly basis;
- normal hours of work and any rules regarding these;
- entitlement to holidays and holiday pay;
- rules on absence due to sickness or injury and any sick pay provided;
- details of any pension scheme and whether the firm has contracted out of the State Pension Scheme;
- the length of notice the employee is entitled to receive and must give;
- the employee's job title.

This may look a rather formidable list, but, when you think about it, these are all fairly obvious things that any reasonable person would want to know before taking a job. You will note also that it does not say what these conditions must be, simply that you have to tell the new employee what conditions you offer.

In deciding upon these, as a new employer, the two guiding principles you should follow are (1) the terms should be competitive, and (2) you should keep it as simple as possible, both to explain and to run. To offer competitive terms, you must find out what other employers do from the same sources as you found out about pay.

To help you choose which practices are best suited to your purpose, rule up a sheet of paper into four vertical columns. In the first column, list the practices under consideration. In the second, put an estimate of the after-tax cost of each item. In the third column, put some comment on the amount of paperwork each is likely to cause. In the last column, put an assessment of how attractive you think each will be for the type of person you want to engage. From such a summary, you should not find it too difficult to select items to form a package which is of reasonable cost, attractive to your employees and simple to run.

Getting applicants

Recruitment is a specialized branch of personnel management and to carry it out in a professional manner requires skills and techniques which are acquired by training and experience. Few readers will already possess such expertise but, by attention to a few basic principles, the new entrepreneur may avoid the major pitfalls and can, with a little practice, achieve an acceptable level of results.

The first step in recruitment is to spell out the job for which the recruit is needed, the kind of person sought and the terms to be offered. Since this has already been covered above, we can move on to the second step, which is to obtain suitable applicants.

Of the various methods of attracting applicants, the most widely used is probably the *old boy network*. You simply spread the word around your family, friends, suppliers and customers in the hope that someone will turn up. One often does – but you can't rely on it. A more positive version is to approach someone who is already working for another employer. This used to be called *poaching* but at the top end of the scale it now goes under the dignified title of *executive search*.

Jobcentres offer a free service and, if you are inexperienced, you may get some helpful advice thrown in. The up-market end, *Professional and Executive Recruitment* (PER), charges a percentage of starting salary. Trained but inexperienced recruits in certain categories may be obtained direct from *schools, colleges and training centres*, provided you can wait until the end of term. Most of these have someone responsible for careers, whom employers can contact. Alternatively, you may approach the *Youth Employ-ment Officer* at your local council. Subsidies or grants are now offered to small businesses engaging certain types of staff – ask your Jobcentre about these.

If you want someone in a hurry – or the above channels seem slow to respond – you may decide to approach a commercial *employment agency*. Many of these specialize in a particular area of employment and, in fact, in some fields (e.g. nursing, catering) these are almost the only really effective way of getting experienced staff. You will need to pay perhaps 5–10 per cent of the annual salary as a commission, although the reputable ones refund this, wholly or partly, if the recruit leaves within a prescribed time. Most of the reputable ones also operate on a 'no recruit – no fee' basis. The disreputable ones do neither – as I know from personal experience – so check on the terms *before* you ask for recruits.

The last but by no means least important method of obtaining applicants is by *advertising*. The cost of this varies enormously, from a few pounds for a classified advertisement in the local press to hundreds of pounds for a display advertisement in the national press. The trade and professional press come in between. The response can vary equally widely – from 'Nil' to several hundred applicants.

If you have an advertising agent, get his advice. If not, try the following. Get the rates, circulation and, if possible, readership breakdown (i.e. proportions by age, sex, social class, etc.) for each of the local papers; just ask them. Study the papers closely, particularly the 'employment vacancies' sections, then decide which one to use. Study the existing advertisements, pick out the ones which look most effective and copy their style.

Selecting staff

Having obtained your applicants, by whatever means, you are now at the third step, viz. to decide which, if any, to engage. If you are not overwhelmed with applicants, you can interview them all. Should you get many applicants, however, you need to do some preliminary screening to cut the number down to a short list of five or six.

If the job requires some skill with paperwork, you can copy the methods of larger firms and send each an application form. This can be a simple duplicated sheet asking for: full name, address, telephone number, marital status, number and age of children; educational and other qualifications; name and address of last three employers, jobs held with dates, commencing and final salary, reason for leaving; name and address and telephone number of two referees; any other information you want.

If paperwork skill is of little consequence in the job, you may screen out the wrong applicants by this means. In this case, you must set up a series of 10–15-minute screening interviews. You may be able to get an experienced friend to help you with these.

It is best to interview short-listed applicants at the workplace, since this gives them a chance to see where they will work, the equipment they will use and perhaps their future colleagues. During the interviews, you need someone to help you, to protect you from any interruption by telephone or persons while you are interviewing, to receive applicants when they arrive and calm them by providing tea or coffee, to pay any travelling expenses incurred and give any directions needed for their return journey.

Most applicants are nervous about interviews and maybe you are too. So start off by explaining about your business and the job you want them to do. This breaks the ice and gives them time to cool off. Then get them talking about familiar subjects. Ask them questions about what they put on the application form, or obtain this information if you have not used one. As they relax, ask more searching questions such as why they want to change jobs or why they have applied to you.

It is your responsibility to control the interview so that you get the information you want. The professional interviewer does this by judicious use of 'closed' and 'open' questions. An over-talkative applicant can be quietened by a rapid succession of 'closed' questions, i.e. questions which require a yes/no answer. A tongue-tied one can be encouraged to loosen up by a series of 'open' questions, e.g. 'What do you like best about your present job?' or 'Tell me something about your hobbies'.

Ask the applicant at the start if he minds if you take notes, so that you do not become confused about different applicants. I have never met anyone who objected. Then take notes quite openly throughout the interview; even experienced interviewers find this essential. Remember also that interviewing is a two-way process. Give the applicant enough time to ask questions and answer them fairly because if you don't, he may not accept the job if you offer it. Moreover, an applicant often reveals a lot about himself by the questions he asks.

It is usually prudent not to tell interviewees, at the time, whether they have been accepted or rejected. You can point out that it is only fair to see all applicants before you decide. You should tell each, however, that you will let them know – either way – within so many days.

Make up your mind quickly and contact the chosen applicant, preferably by telephone, to offer him the job, subject to obtaining satisfactory references. If he accepts, the referees should be approached immediately, again preferably by telephone and, if they report satisfactorily, you should confirm the job offer in writing, asking for a written acceptance by return.

Within the agreed time, rejected applicants should be sent

a polite letter, thanking them for coming for interview, but saying that another applicant was considered more suitable. Occasionally a rejected applicant may write or telephone to ask why. If this happens, simply repeat that in your judgement another applicant was more suitable and that you are not prepared to discuss the matter further. If you allow yourself to be drawn into a discussion, there is a risk that an incautious remark could be quoted out of context and used to claim unlawful discrimination (see Chapter 19). So play it safe.

At the end of the interviews, you may feel that none of the applicants is suitable. If so, resist the temptation to take the best of a bad bunch, rather than go through all that again. All that is likely to happen is that you hire someone, have an unsatisfactory work experience, then go through the hassle of firing him. Then you *still* have to go through all that again. Better sooner than later. Look again at the pay and conditions of employment you offer and the methods used to get applicants. Change them if necessary and start again.

Managing staff

Many entrepreneurs are afraid to hire staff these days because of the difficulties created by recent employment laws. It is true that life has become more complicated for employers but the reality is not as bad as many think it is. Otherwise there would not be thousands of businesses still surviving and prospering. These laws are discussed more fully in Chapter 19, from which you will see that many do not apply to small businesses, to part-time staff or to newly engaged employees. As was pointed out at the beginning of this chapter, if your business is to succeed, you will need to engage staff at some stage. So take heart – and start to learn how to manage staff so as to get the best out of them.

Some people are born with the gift of managing others but most of us have to learn from experience – our own and that of others. In your previous work, you have probably known a number of bosses. Think about them in retrospect. Which bosses did you admire? What qualities did they show that made you and others respect them? Which bosses did you think were poor? What qualities did you dislike in them? By examining your experience in this way, you can decide which qualities to foster in yourself and what mistakes to avoid.

In your journey through memory, try to distinguish between these bosses' behaviour as people and as managers. You can like someone very much as a person and yet recognize that he is a poor manager. Similarly, you can dislike someone and yet admit, perhaps reluctantly, that he is a good manager. In managing your staff, your aim is not to be 'liked'. If you achieve this it is a bonus, but it is not the first consideration. Your aim is to be 'respected', provided you do not arouse active dislike.

Most staff will respond to honesty, fair treatment, respect as an individual, kindness – and firmness. But this firmness must be consistent, not of the 'blow hot – blow cold' variety, and must be the same for all – no favouritism. The behaviour you want from them in return will depend upon your type of business.

Some businesses require fairly strict discipline, because it is needed to satisfy customers, just as others require relaxed conditions, for the same reason. But discipline does not mean you should try to rule with a rod of iron, because competent staff will not accept that today. Similarly, informality should not degenerate into sloppiness.

It is your responsibility as the owner of the business to decide upon the 'atmosphere' needed for your business, to select staff who will work well in such surroundings and to handle them in a manner which produces it. Never forget that running a business is not a popularity contest – it is an economic activity.

CHAPTER 17

The Customer is King

Each chapter in this book deals with an aspect of starting a business which is important. You have to choose the right business, one which suits your abilities and for which there is a market. You have to assemble the right resources in financial, material and human terms and you have to tackle the process of starting it in the right way. But these are of no avail if you do not get that ingredient vital to all business success – customers.

In your other life, as a customer, you may think that you choose where and what to buy. But just ask yourself *why* you choose to approach a particular business for your goods or services. Is it because you have had satisfactory dealings there before? Is it because friends have recommended it? Is it because you have seen it advertised? Is it because it is located conveniently – or the quality is better – or the prices are lower – or what?

All these things can be influenced by the business owner. The purpose of this chapter is to discuss the factors which cause a customer to choose one business rather than another and to show how you can get customers for *your* business.

What are you selling?

You may think the answer to this question is obvious – let us say 'groceries'. But this is only half an answer, which needs to be taken a little further. Consider the answers given by Les, Peter and David.

Les says: 'I run a mini-market, stocking a full range of basic foodstuffs, in the middle of a working-class suburb in the North East. I belong to a voluntary buying chain, my rent is low and I reckon I can price as keenly as the big supermarket chains in the centre of town. And customers don't have to pay shocking bus fares or parking fees to come to my shop.'

Peter says: 'I own a high-class grocery shop in a market town in the South West. I stock a wide range of good-quality foods, including wines and a delicatessen. Mine may not be the cheapest shop in town, but it's the only one where you can get certain things. What is more, I still offer a delivery service to the surrounding villages.'

David says: 'I have a village store in East Anglia. The local bus service is infrequent and expensive, so many villagers prefer to shop with me, even if I'm not as cheap as the town supermarkets. They have to buy a lot in town to save their fares. Besides I like to have a chat with my customers – I've known most of them since I was a lad. Sometimes I'm the only person they talk to for days on end.'

Do you get the point? You don't just sell groceries. You sell a particular range of groceries at a particular price level. You also supply a particular service, whether it be 'a supermarket on the doorstep', 'high quality with all the trimmings' or 'a chance for a chat'. You must get a very clear picture of what you are selling firmly fixed in your mind.

Type of customer

As already mentioned in Chapter 2, you must decide at an early stage the type of customer you cater for. All of the businesses mentioned above are selling direct to the public but, as you well know, this is by no means the rule. There are other types of customer and the methods which attract one type may not be appropriate for another.

When selling to the *public*, your premises must, in general, be well-lit and decorated in a pleasing fashion. Location may be critical, since many customers put great store on convenience. Consequently, if you want to induce people to come from a distance to your premises, you must have a strong counter-attraction. This may be very low prices, a wide range of stock, easy parking, free delivery, goods not available elsewhere, flexible opening hours or a combination of these.

When selling to *commercial or industrial companies*, different considerations apply. In the first place, customers may rarely if ever visit the premises, so appearance is less important. Location may still matter, but from a distribution-cost standpoint, not the convenience of the travelling public. Purchasing decisions are likely to be made by technical specialists or professional buyers, rather than laymen. Consequently, although salesmanship is still important, more weight may be put on such factors as product quality, delivery time, price and terms of payment. Moreover, each individual order may be of much greater value and require more effort to secure.

Similar factors may prevail when selling to *government departments*. There is also a greater likelihood of having to tender for a product specified by the customer rather than sell one's own branded product, and packaging becomes utilitarian rather than possessing customer appeal. One may also have to submit samples or permit inspection before dispatch. Contracts may be for very large quantities phased over a period of time. Cost inflation can erode future profits from such contracts, unless provision is made for corresponding escalation of price, and fixed-price contracts must be treated with caution.

Local and regional authorities occupy an intermediate position between the above two categories. The larger authorities may use tendering and inspection procedures similar to those of government departments since their purchases are on a similar scale. The smaller authorities behave more like private-sector companies. Recent scandals have made some wary about laying themselves open to charges of bribery and corruption, which may sometimes make it difficult to establish personal relations with purchasing officers. On the other hand, most councils are anxious to encourage local enterprises, provided this incurs no extra cost for the ratepayer.

Another point which must be considered is whether your 'customer' is the *ultimate consumer* or a middleman. Do you sell your products to a retailer or wholesaler who, in turn, sells them to the consumer? Are you a sub-contractor, providing only part of the final product? Are you paid by some agency to provide a service to a third party?

If your business is of this nature, you must find some means of getting 'feedback' from the ultimate consumer. What are their real needs? What do they really think about the goods or service you provide? This may be obtained by market research, by consumer surveys, by salesmen's reports or by a combination of these. It is dangerous to rely solely upon the information you get from the middleman since, by ignorance or design, this may be misleading.

Methods of selling

The type of customer you aim for will affect the method of selling you adopt. The most popular method for a small business is face to face, direct to the ultimate customer, as in a shop, market stall or delivery van. Its counterpart with a service is where you go round, knocking on doors and inviting people to use your service. This method appeals to the extrovert and is particularly appropriate where the goods or services are not in themselves unique and the success of the business depends mainly upon energetic selling.

An alternative method of selling direct to the consumer is by mail order. You may advertise specific items in the press or invite orders from a catalogue, either directly or through a network of agents. Such a venture may be run from your home or factory, which saves the rent of a shop. It may also appeal to entrepreneurs who lack confidence in their ability to sell face to face. Mail order is particularly appropriate for goods which possess some unique quality, where demand is widely scattered or where your business is primarily manufacturing rather than selling.

There are still other methods such as: renting a small space within a store where your goods are displayed and sold by your employee (shop within a shop); placing goods in a shop for sale on commission; door-to-door sales representatives (e.g. Kleen-E-Ze brushes); part-time sales representatives (e.g. Avon cosmetics); household parties at which goods are demonstrated (e.g. Tupperware).

Manufacturing concerns frequently sell their products not to consumers but to wholesalers or retailers. This enables them to sell in large batches to a limited number of outlets, the lower selling price being offset by reduced selling expenses. Goods can also be sold in large batches to company or public-sector buyers or you can submit tenders for goods made to the buyer's specification. Finally, you may rely upon independent agents to sell your products on a commission basis.

Getting customers – the indirect way

In the beginning, few people will know that your business exists. Building up a clientele by word of mouth recommendation is a slow process – slower than many new businesses can afford. It is therefore customary to accelerate this process by *sales promotion*.

Planning a sales promotion campaign is a stepwise operation, of which the first step is to define the *target* at which your promotion will be aimed. Within the type of customer you have chosen, can you identify a sector which contains a high proportion of potential customers? Are business customers most likely to be found in organizations of a particular type, size, industrial sector and geographical area? Can your 'typical' individual customer be described in terms of age, sex, social class, occupational group, etc.? The more closely you can define your target the more effective will be your promotion.

What is the *message* you want to convey to your target? It is not enough just to make them aware of your product or service; you must also make them want to buy it. Look at it through their eyes. Does it make them feel good? Does it provide an easier or better way of doing something? Does it enable them to do something they couldn't do before? Does it allow them to avoid doing something they dislike?

Even if they want what you offer, why should they buy it from you and not your competitor? Is yours better – or cheaper – or in some way unique? What action should they take if they want to buy from you? You must condense all of the above into two or three clear and concise sentences to form your message.

What are the best means of communicating your message to your target? In short, which *media* should you use? In recent years, 'media' has come to be regarded as meaning press, TV and radio but this is too narrow a view for our purpose. You must also consider other media, e.g. posters; leaflets (distributed door-to-door or inserted in magazines); mailing shots; bus, train and tube advertising; trade directories; Yellow Pages and any others you can think of.

Prepare a short list of those which seem appropriate and compare them in terms of coverage of target; suitability for the message; probable effectiveness; cost. Unless you are experienced in this field, you will probably need the help of an advertising agent in assessing these. Then choose the package which seems to give the best results for your budget.

Before going into action, you must decide upon *timing*. Is all of the money you budgeted available at the start or does cash flow restrict spending at certain times? Should you make a big splash at the start or run a sustained campaign? Once again the advice of a good advertising agent is invaluable, but remember that he may be biased towards spending in certain ways.

Getting customers – the direct way

There is a temptation for many new entrepreneurs to rely overmuch on 'sales promotion' rather than 'salesmanship', particularly when they have had no previous sales experience. They persuade themselves that, with the first-class product and excellent service they offer, there is no need for all that high-pressure stuff. 'Good wine needs no bush', they quote.

In many cases they are being dishonest; they won't admit to themselves that they lack the courage to approach a stranger and ask him to buy. They foster an image of the salesman as being 'brash' or 'smooth' – they don't want to be like that. Secretly they are afraid.

You must realize that sales promotion is a method of preparing the ground, but unless it is followed up by active salesmanship the results will be small. Advertising may cause someone to enter your shop but you still have to sell once he gets there, or else he may go out empty-handed – and never return. A mailing shot may make potential customers aware of your sub-contracting business but unless you follow up with a personal approach, you will be forgotten by the time they need your services.

Have you ever wondered why good salesmen are well paid? It is because selling is difficult and few people learn to do it really well. Of course some have great natural talent but most people can learn to do it competently.

Some entrepreneurs start what is potentially a good business, run a good sales-promotion campaign and then sit back waiting for customers. When they don't appear, the entrepreneur bemoans his bad luck or the stupidity of customers. Some such entrepreneurs go bust. Desperation finally drives others to put on their coats and go knocking

on doors. To their surprise, they get a pleasant reception
from most people they approach and – more important –
some orders.

Don't wait until the bank manager complains about your
mounting overdraft and you are 'living off the shop' or
laying off the staff you trained so carefully. Don't wait until
desperation overcomes your fear. Go out looking for customers from the start. Of course this takes courage, but
starting a business *does* take courage. If you haven't got
courage, you shouldn't start a business.

Plan your direct approach along the same lines as your
promotion campaign. Choose your *target* with care, to increase your chances of success. Prepare your *message* beforehand; rehearse your sales patter by getting a patient
spouse or friend to play the role of reluctant customer.
Choose your *media*, e.g. telephone call, written request for
an appointment, unannounced call, etc. Watch the *timing* –
try to keep your direct approach in step with your promotion campaign for maximum impact.

There is much sympathy today for the new entrepreneur
and you will probably get a better reception than you
expect. Even if someone can't buy, he may suggest another
who can. The worst that can happen is that someone shuts
the door in your face. So what! Go to the next on the list and
keep going till you get those orders.

Follow through

If you are inexperienced, things may go wrong with your
efforts to get customers. You may forget something – overlook something – make wrong decisions. Don't fret if these
things happen because this is the price you have to pay to
gain experience. It is not fatal, provided you pick them up
quickly and take corrective action. In short, you must follow
through.

Measure your volume of business frequently, both number of customers and size of order. Try to assess how much additional business is produced by each promotional activity. There are many tricks you can use: code references in advertisements; different-coloured leaflets for different distributions; reply coupons, Freepost or reply-paid cards. Study what other businesses do, copy the good ideas and avoid the mistakes. Above all, don't be afraid to ask customers why they came to you.

Hold regular post-mortem sessions with your advertising agent to review the results of past campaigns. See what lessons you can learn and apply them to future campaigns. Don't be afraid to admit mistakes – profit from them – don't repeat them.

In the beginning, all of your customers are new ones, but gradually the proportion of 'repeat business' builds up. This will vary from one type of business to another; it will obviously be much higher in groceries than double-glazing. But even if an old customer does not need to buy again soon, if he is satisfied he will recommend you to his friends. This indirect form of repeat business can be stimulated by various incentives.

Measure periodically how much of your trade is from new customers and how much from old and use this to guide future strategy. If new business is dropping off, you may need to freshen up your promotion. If the volume of repeat business stops rising or drops, look at your business methods. Has the quality of your product or service dropped? Are you charging too much? Has a new competitor entered the field? Have you – or your staff – stopped trying so hard?

Another way of assessing progress is by the number and type of complaints. Make sure that all complaints are reported to you and as far as possible deal with them personally. This means you must be much more severe with an employee who conceals a complaint than with one who causes a complaint. Of course you must also take steps to ensure it doesn't happen again.

To the complaining customers you should be generous – even over-generous – because then they will tell all their friends how nicely you treated them. This is a more effective, and probably cheaper, form of promotion than paid advertising. Thank the customer for giving you the opportunity to put it right. Don't argue with him. You are trying to win more business – not a debate. And don't ever forget – or let your staff forget – that *the customer is king*!

CHAPTER 18

As Others See Us

When I was a child, a local dry cleaner had a poster in his window, quoting from Robert Burns:

> O wad some power the giftie gie us,
> To see ourselves as others see us.

Beneath this poster stood a large mirror. The purpose of this chapter is to help you construct such a mirror, so that you can see yourself, and to describe methods by which you can influence how others see you.

Why bother?

Because your business has an 'image', whether you realize it or not. Consciously or unconsciously, other people are forming opinions about your business from the many impressions they receive; how you behave when you speak or write to them; the style of your advertising; the quality of the products or service you provide; the appearance of your premises, delivery equipment, packages and stationery; the way your staff treat them; the prices you charge; your reliability in fulfilling promises; and so on.

The opinions they form will, in turn, affect how they behave to you. The disgruntled customer who feels that he has been badly treated is unlikely to buy more – and will tell others of your shortcomings. The creditor who has to chase you to get his money will try to avoid being your creditor in future. People who visit a seedy, rundown workplace will think it is occupied by a seedy, rundown business. Neighbours who find your business spoils their 'quality of life' will complain and may even try to close it down.

You may feel, of course, that these are simply arguments for running a business efficiently, so that you avoid a bad reputation. But the reasons for looking at your image are positive as well as negative. If you can get a lot of satisfied customers, suppliers and neighbours talking enthusiastically about what a good business it is, others will hear of it. You will not only avoid a bad reputation, you will gain a good one. Moreover, if a slip occurs – as it does with everyone at some stage – it is more likely to be accepted as an aberration rather than as typical.

In short, it is not enough to run a business well – essential though that is – you must be seen to run it well. If an image of some kind is going to be attached to your business, isn't it worth taking a little trouble to ensure it is the one you want?

Choosing the right image

What kind of image do you want? It is not enough to answer, 'A good one'. There are many different kinds of image which are good in the sense that they are socially acceptable, but they may not be appropriate for *your* business. For instance, if you are trying to promote a stream-lined, efficient service in a field which is highly price-competitive, it is not very helpful to get a reputation as a firm with high-quality products and relaxed, friendly staff.

The answer to the above question must be derived from your business strategy. What kind of business are you in? What kind of goods or service do you offer? What class of market are you aiming for – high quality, low price or intermediate? Are you offering a wide product range or a narrow specialized one? What type of customer are you particularly trying to attract?

You can begin to see the kind of image which goes with the business you are trying to create. It is sometimes helpful to make a list of adjectives which you think are appropriate.

Try to get at least a dozen, referring to a dictionary or thesaurus if necessary. From this list, pick out the three most important ones.

The image chosen must fit your personality, since you are the one who must put it across. If you adopt an individualistic style, so much the better. To many people, one of the attractions of dealing with small businesses is the colourful character of the owner. It goes without saying that any personality you display must be genuine. Anything 'phoney' will be uncomfortable to live with and, sooner or later, will be detected.

Creating an image

To achieve the maximum effectiveness in fostering an image, you need to apply consistency and consonance. *Consistency* means that you should promote the same image over a considerable period of time. Although the way it is presented may vary from time to time, the message should remain unchanged.

Consonance means that the same image should be presented through all the different means available – the behaviour of your staff and yourself, quality and price of product or service, appearance of your workplace and vehicles, design of stationery and advertising, etc. Different means may emphasize different aspects but there should be an underlying unity.

All businesses require to meet a minimum standard in matters such as cleanliness, courtesy, cost-consciousness, etc. How far you go above the minimum will depend not only upon the nature of the business but also upon the image desired. The standard of cleanliness needed in a food store is obviously higher than in, say, a hardware shop but even within the category of food stores one encounters some which are positively 'gleaming' while others are just 'acceptable'. Similarly, in clothing shops the luxury boutique might place the main emphasis on 'courtesy' and the discount draper on 'cost-consciousness'.

Achieving and keeping the high standard necessary in your key qualities depends greatly upon how your staff behave. Naturally you will take this into account when selecting staff but it must be constantly reinforced by training and example. This task can be made easier by careful design and layout of the workplace and by the business methods adopted.

In recent years, a branch of consultancy has sprung up, dealing with what is called 'visible manifestations'. Somehow the term always makes me think of ghosts but it relates to all those outward appearances of a company which are visible to the public, e.g. shops, office buildings, delivery and service vehicles, advertisements of all kinds, trademarks, stationery, product packaging, staff uniforms, etc. To be fair, a large multinational company probably needs an outside consultant to achieve some degree of worldwide uniformity.

Fortunately for you, the small business does not need a consultant but the point should not be overlooked. When choosing designs for any of the things mentioned above, the entrepreneur should always ask two questions: (1) which design will best promote the desired image? (2) which design fits in best with existing 'visible manifestations'? Many quite small businesses find it worth while adopting a logotype and a standard colour scheme as aids to promoting a consistent image.

The good neighbour

New enterprises can be uncomfortable neighbours. They may cause smells or fumes which some people dislike. (Even a perfume factory can produce unpleasant odours in the immediate vicinity.) They may emit a noise level which, although normal by industrial standards, is intolerable to the inhabitants of a quiet residential area. The constant to and fro of supply and delivery vehicles may cause noise, fumes, congestion and fear for the safety of children. Consequently, it is hardly suprising that the attitude of many residents towards a new business is the same as that towards prisons and mental institutions, 'Of course we must have them – but not here!'

The new entrepreneur must therefore ensure that the premises, equipment and methods he uses will not cause offence to his neighbours. It is not enough just to meet minimum legal requirements if existing residents have been accustomed to much higher standards. It is much easier and cheaper to avoid setting up somewhere than to be forced to move afterwards. Even if you are thinking of starting up in your own garage or backyard, make sure that neighbours' complaints will not force the local council to withhold planning permission for 'change of use'.

If the entrepreneur oversteps the mark, he may find that his neighbours may harass him in ways which are not only unpleasant but interfere with operations. Employees may be put under pressure to leave their jobs. Lorry drivers may face hostile demonstrations on entering and leaving the workplace. Moreover, such feeling can sometimes be whipped up by a local politician or newspaper reporter for reasons of personal ambition.

Creating a good image with the neighbours is not just a matter of avoiding inconvenience. Positive steps can be taken to overcome apprehension. Why not start the business with a housewarming party for the neighbours – in the factory? A little unorthodoxy or even cheek is usually well taken from the new enterprise starting on a shoestring. Decorate the outside of your premises in a manner which enhances the appearance of the neighbourhood. Say it with flowers – even if it is only window-boxes.

Think too of the surrounding community. Is there an inexpensive but appropriate gift you can make to a local hospital, school or community centre? What about an annual 'birthday party' for old-age pensioners to mark the anniversary of your opening? Regular reading of the local papers will provide ideas for things you can do for the community. What matters is not how much you spend but the thought which goes into how you spend it. Gradually you can build up the feeling among the populace that your business is an asset to them in more than economic terms.

Handling the media

The image-promoters discussed so far have all been more or less under the control of the entrepreneur. When it comes to 'the media', which are largely outside his control, most entrepreneurs 'adopt a low profile', 'play it cool' or follow whatever euphemism they prefer for 'do nothing'. Such an attitude is very understandable – but it is not necessarily the best one. I say this even though I have had personal experience of my utterances being distorted, quoted out of context and generally used as a stick to beat me.

If one does come under fire from the media, the best defence is not attack. This can so often backfire and land one even deeper in the mire. The best defence is what the police call 'previous good conduct'. If you have taken the trouble to cultivate a good image people are less likely to believe allegations against you. Moreover, if you are known to have a good reputation, the scurrilous are less likely to attack you. They will seek easier targets.

You will be in a very strong position if you have taken the trouble to make friends with responsible journalists. They can be supplied with information which they can use to rebut the allegations. Nor is this the only reason for establishing good relations right from the start, particularly with the local press. Reporters are always short of good copy and if you can supply them with news of interesting happenings, they will be grateful. You can get free and favourable publicity in this way and bring your business to the notice of a wider range of potential customers.

There is no need to limit your sights to the local press. Local radio and regional TV are also on the lookout for local events to report. The national press and many magazines run features on new products and services and sometimes on new businesses. They may give you a brief write-up or even do a feature on your business. It only costs a phone call or a letter to try.

The trade press is often overlooked by the new entrepreneur. Nevertheless, it is the most effective medium for becoming better known 'in the trade', thus gaining the respect of both suppliers and competitors. Make sure that the appropriate magazines are kept informed of your activities, bearing in mind the long lead time of monthly publications. So give them plenty of notice, if necessary putting an 'embargo' on the information supplied if you don't want it published before a certain date. And don't restrict yourself to news items. Why not try writing the occasional article on a topic of trade interest? There is no better way of establishing a sound professional image.

In one start-up of a new factory in which I was involved, one of the staff started to keep a scrapbook of all the press cuttings which referred to the enterprise – both favourable and unfavourable. During the early months, this helped us to sort out friend from foe among the press. It proved interesting to visitors and was a useful source of ammunition to rebut some unfair criticism. You may like to copy the idea.

CHAPTER 19

The Businessman and the Law

The reader cannot help but be aware of the flood of legislation which has appeared in the past ten years, concerning the rights of consumers and employees. Much of this was well-intentioned but, unfortunately, some has not achieved its intended effects and some has had effects which were not intended. Not only has the number of laws enacted been much greater than ever before experienced in this country but the details of some have seesawed back and forth with successive changes in government. To add to the burden, there has been a stream of rules and regulations as a consequence of joining the EEC and more than usual fluctuations in methods and rates of taxation.

In response to this situation, would-be entrepreneurs have reacted in several ways. Some have decided to 'press on regardless'. They just ignore it all and, for a time, may be successful. Sooner or later, however, they will run into trouble. If it is serious, their business may founder; if they extricate themselves, they may be consumed with worry about what other pitfalls await them. At the other extreme, some may try to learn all about the laws and become DIY legal experts. They soon learn that this is a pursuit which even professional lawyers find difficult and which leaves them little time to run their business.

Throughout all this period, hundreds of thousands of people have continued to run businesses and every year thousands more join their ranks. Life has undoubtedly become more difficult but they survive and remain sane. How do they do it? They learn enough to be able to comply with the laws which affect their day-to-day operations and to detect when they need professional advice to cope with possible trouble. The purpose of this chapter is to help the reader join the 'survivors'.

Finding out

The first task is, of course, to find out which laws affect you and for this you naturally turn to your professional advisers. This greatly increased output of new laws has obviously affected them too. The accountant can no longer simply churn out annual audits nor can the solicitor confine himself to probate, conveyancing and divorce. Any who do are of little value to the entrepreneur. In choosing a professional adviser, you must take care to select one with a sound knowledge of the laws which affect your business – and who keeps himself up-to-date.

In Chapter 8, the importance was stressed of establishing an ongoing relationship with your professional advisers. A good foundation for this is to arrange a detailed discussion to clarify which laws apply to your business and how you can best comply with them. Probably your accountant will advise on taxation and financial legislation and your solicitor on the rest but the precise fields of interest must be sorted out between you.

In addition to a preliminary briefing from your professional advisers, you need to acquire a working knowledge of the laws which most affect your business. It is not practicable – besides being expensive – to ring up your solicitor for every little problem which arises through the day. Consequently, you need to supplement the professional advice you are given by self-education. This can be done by reading, using cassettes or by attending lectures, training courses or seminars.

In choosing methods of self-education, various considerations apply. First is availability; books and articles exist about every aspect of legislation but other methods are limited in their coverage. Second is suitability for you. Some people are 'visual' learners, i.e. they learn best by reading, looking at pictures and diagrams and watching someone do something. Others are 'aural' learners, i.e. they learn best by listening to someone explaining it, either in the flesh or on records, film or tape.

Third is appropriateness for the subject. Some aspects of legislation are logical, factual and clear-cut and can be learned by solitary study. Other aspects are partly subjective, requiring judgement to interpret; these are better learned by lectures and discussion. Finally one must consider how much time and money can be allocated to what is only a part – although an important part – of starting a business.

You can find out what methods are available for particular laws from the sources of advice given in Appendix 2. Having chosen your methods, you must then draw up a study programme which is realistic in terms of the time you can spare.

Once you have done your initial study, you need to keep up-to-date because this is a continually changing scene. Your advisers should tell you about developments which affect you, which is why they need a good understanding of your business. It is prudent, however, to supplement this by keeping a close watch on the newspapers, trade magazines and the bulletins from your trade association.

There are also several systematic methods of keeping informed. One which I have found relatively painless is to belong to Consumers' Association. The monthly magazine *Which* reports changes in consumer law and important case judgements. To a lesser extent it also covers employment law. These articles are of course written from the viewpoint of the consumer and employee.

Another book which I recommend, written from the entrepreneur's viewpoint, is *Reference Book for the Self Employed and Smaller Business* issued by Croner Publications

Ltd. Not only does this give a concise summary of most of the laws affecting new businesses but the annual subscription includes a monthly updating service.

As an employer, you are responsible for what your sales staff say to customers, the advice they offer, the promises they make and the guarantees they give, even if not in writing. If your staff do work or service equipment on customers' premises, you must ensure that they do it properly. As a manufacturer, you are responsible for the quality of your products and for carrying out any inspection necessary to maintain this quality.

These responsibilities may involve you in training your staff. Much of this training will be done by example, by how you behave on the job, but it is sometimes necessary to supplement this by more systematic methods. Many equipment manufacturers run training courses for service staff. Trade associations and industry training boards sometimes have 'packaged training kits' which you can obtain and some even provide instructors.

The way in which the law affects each entrepreneur varies so much with the nature and scope of the business that it is impossible to give specific advice. The rest of this chapter gives a brief outline of some of the more common laws to give you a rough idea of what may affect you. *I would stress, however, the importance of checking with your own professional advisers precisely where you and your business stand regarding the law.*

Taxation and accounts

As already mentioned in Chapter 5, if you run your business as a sole trader or partnership, your profits will be subject to personal *income tax* under Schedule D. A description of how this works in the first few years is given in Chapter 14.

If you form a limited company, the profits of that

company will be subject to *corporation tax*. Your accountant should assist you in dealing with this. He or your solicitor should also advise you on the statutory requirements under *company law* to which you must conform, e.g. holding of Annual General Meeting, issue of Annual Accounts and Directors' Report and sending of Annual Return to the Registrar of Companies.

Most goods and services are subject to *Value Added Tax* (*VAT*). At the time of writing, you are legally obliged to notify Customs and Excise if your turnover (N.B. turnover not profit) has exceeded £6000 in the past quarter or £18,000 in the past year. You must do this within 10 days of the end of the quarter. Furthermore, if you have reasonable grounds for believing that your turnover will exceed £18,000 in the next twelve months, then you are also obliged to give notification. These figures are changed fairly frequently, so check on the latest ones. If you expect your turnover will be less than £18,000 per annum, you need do nothing.

Even if you are not legally obliged, it is worth considering whether you should register. If you are not registered, you cannot recover VAT paid on your purchases. Non-registration also advertises the fact that your annual turnover is below £18,000. VAT can also help your cash flow, since you collect it over three months and then repay it one month in arrears. If you are in doubt, you can discuss it at your local VAT office (listed in the telephone directory under Customs & Excise Department). On request, the VAT office will send a representative to look over the account system you are proposing to set up and tell you if it is suitable.

It is the duty of an employer to deduct tax due under *Pay As You Earn* (*PAYE*) from the pay of the employees, whether or not he has been directed to do so by the Inland Revenue. This is done by the use of Tax Tables supplied to employers by the Inland Revenue. Full details of how the scheme is operated are given in the current edition of the

Employer's Guide to PAYE which can be obtained from your local tax office. Employers are normally not required to deduct PAYE from self-employed workers but there is one important exception. In the construction industry, contractors are obliged to deduct tax from sub-contractors who do not hold a valid 'certificate of exemption'.

It is also the duty of employers to deduct *earnings-related National Insurance (NI) Class 1 contributions* from the income of employees. This is closely integrated with the PAYE deduction system since, with a few exceptions (e.g. pension contributions), the same income figure is used for both deductions.

Legal requirements and the returns you make to government departments influence the records you must keep. Hence you must find out what these are and take them into account when designing your record system. While some allowance for possible future changes might be made, this should not be taken to the point of undue complexity.

Employment laws

The *Factories Act 1961* applies to premises which are defined as 'factories' within the Act – a much wider definition than popular usage suggests. Any person who proposes to occupy premises as a factory must give at least one month's written notice of their intention to the District Inspector.

At the staff entrances to factories, various abstracts and notices must be posted. Many regulations are laid down regarding: conditions of work, records of persons employed (particularly women and young persons), holidays, use of machinery, reporting of industrial accidents, first aid facilities, welfare, etc.

The *Offices, Shops and Railway Premises Act 1963* lays down regulations covering offices and shop premises regarding: canteens, light and ventilation, sanitation, seating facilities, machinery, notification of accidents, etc. This Act does not apply to premises where only self-employed people work, where the employees are close relations of the employer, where outworkers work in their own homes, where the total hours worked on the premises by all employees does not normally exceed 21 hours per week or where the premises are occupied for not more than six weeks.

The *Shops Act 1950* is mainly concerned with the hours of work of shop assistants. It requires that each shop assistant should have a weekly half-holiday and lays down rules for meal intervals and work on Sundays. Special regulations apply to licensed premises and shops in holiday resorts.

The *Health and Safety at Work Act 1974* places the duty on every employer to ensure the health and safety and welfare at work of all his employees, so far as is reasonably practicable. An employer with five or more employees must prepare a written statement of his general policy on this matter and the arrangement set up to carry out the policy and bring it to the notice of employees. This Act applies to every firm, however small, to employers and employees and to the self-employed. Regulations and revisions will continue to be issued in future years.

The *Fire Precautions Act 1971* makes provision for the protection of persons from fire risks while on factory, office or shop premises or in hotels or boarding houses. A fire certificate is required for factory, office or shop premises in which more than twenty persons are employed, or in which more than ten persons are employed other than on the ground floor, or in which explosive or highly inflammable materials are stored or used. The Act applies to hotels and boarding houses with sleeping accommodation for more than six (including staff and guests) or with any sleeping accommodation (staff or guests) above the first floor or below the ground floor. Some of the regulations apply to all factory, office and shop premises in which any persons are employed.

The *Employment Protection (Consolidation) Act 1978* consolidated the legislation contained in Redundancy Payments Act 1965, Contracts of Employment Act 1972, Trade Union and Labour Relations Acts 1974 and 1976 and the Employment Protection Act 1975. In its turn, the 1978 Act has been amended by the *Employment Acts of 1980 and 1982* and a further Act is now under discussion. Even the existing laws are subject to re-interpretation as case law is created by the slow process of judgement, appeal and counter-appeal.

Most of the recent changes relate to the *collective rights* of employees and under these continually changing conditions there is no point in my trying to describe the state of the law at the moment of writing. It will probably be different by the time you read this, so you will need up-to-date professional advice in any case.

The majority of new businesses do not have enough employees to encounter this problem in their early days. What does, however, concern any new business as soon as it has even one employee, even part-time, is the *individual rights* of employees. Fortunately these have changed little since the passage of the individual Acts which were consolidated in 1978, and the more important points are summarized below:

Redundancy – All employees who have been continuously employed for two years or more after the age of 18 are entitled to receive payment in the event of being made redundant. This applies to almost all businesses, however small, but not to self-employed staff. Provided all the requirements are met, the employer may claim 41 per cent of the official redundancy payment (but not any additional payments).

Contract of employment – As described in Chapter 16, all employees working 16 or more hours per week must receive a written statement or contract of employment not later than 13 weeks after starting employment.

Employment protection – Applies to all firms, even those with only one employee, and to part-time as well as full-time staff. The many provisions include: guarantee payments during lay-offs or short time; maternity leave; right of employee to receive written reasons for dismissal; right of employee to time off with or without pay for trade union activities or public duties; prevention of discrimination or victimization for union membership or activities. In many cases the employer may be obliged to appear before an industrial tribunal to answer the complaint against him.

Trade union and labour relations – Covers every employee, regardless of size of firm, who has been continuously employed for 16 hours per week or more for a period of 26 weeks or for 8 hours per week or more for at least five years. Establishes the rights of such an employee not to be unfairly dismissed, entitles him to present a complaint to an industrial tribunal if he considers he has been dismissed unfairly and specifies reasons for which dismissal will be treated as unfair. If the reasons for dismissal are associated with trade union membership or activities, the Act applies even if the employee has worked less than 26 weeks.

The *Employers' Liability (Compulsory Insurance) Act 1969* and later amendments require employers to insure employees against bodily injury or disease arising from employment, under an approved policy with an authorized insurer. The employer is also required to display a copy of the certificate of insurance at the workplace.

The *Sex Discrimination Act 1975* and the *Race Relations Act 1976*, together with some provisions of the Acts quoted above, make it unlawful for an employer to discriminate against applicants for jobs on grounds of sex, race or trade union affiliation. Care must be taken in wording advertisements and in the treatment of applicants to avoid laying yourself open to complaint from a disappointed applicant.

Hence the advice in Chapter 16 to play it safe. These Acts also apply after engagement and employers must not discriminate in pay, conditions of employment, access to training, promotion, etc.

The above brief outline presents a picture which you may find rather intimidating. In the opinion of many employers, the dice are loaded heavily against them. Nevertheless, these Acts must be observed if you want to keep on the right side of the law. As a new entrepreneur, what can you do?

There are various measures you can take to avoid or minimize legal complications. You may keep the business in the family, engage staff on a self-employed basis, use contract services or casual labour. But sooner or later most successful businesses have to hire employees. This is one of the 'penalties of success', so don't be too down-hearted about it. With reasonable care in selection and treatment, your new employee can help to make your business even more successful.

Consumer Laws

The *Sale of Goods Act 1979* consolidated and largely replaced the earlier Acts regulating contracts of sale of goods, in particular *Sale of Goods Act 1893*, *Misrepresentation Act 1967* and *Supply of Goods (Implied Terms) Act 1973*. In a contract of sale of goods, the seller transfers, or agrees to transfer, goods to the buyer for a price. A contract may be made in writing, by word of mouth, or implied from the conduct of the parties concerned. It is the duty of the seller to deliver the goods and of the buyer to accept and pay for them in accordance with the terms of the contract.

Unless otherwise agreed, the goods remain at the seller's risk until ownership is transferred, when they will be at the buyer's risk – whether delivery has been made or not. If delivery is delayed through the fault of either buyer or seller, the goods will be at the risk of whoever is at fault.

Under the *Trade Descriptions Act 1968*, it is a criminal offence to make a statement, which is known to be false, in respect of goods or services offered. This applies to oral statements as well as to those in writing. A statement published in a book, newspaper or magazine is not regarded as a trade description unless it forms part of an advertisement. Anyone indicating that goods are being offered at a price lower than the actual price will be guilty of an offence.

The *Consumer Protection Act 1961* stipulates that no one may sell, or have in his possession for the purpose of selling, any goods or component parts covered by regulations made under this Act unless the requirements of these regulations are met. Regulations have been issued for a wide range of goods.

The *Sex Discrimination Act 1975* and *Race Relations Act 1976* apply to the provision of goods, facilities and services as well as to employment. It is therefore unlawful to discriminate on grounds of sex or race by refusing or deliberately neglecting to provide goods, facilities or services offered to the public or by refusing or deliberately neglecting to provide them on the same terms and conditions as are offered to other members of the public.

The best protection against the consumer laws is to provide goods and services of satisfactory quality. This must be supported by careful wording of advertisements, sales-promotion material and contracts and by thorough training of sales staff. In some types of business, you can obtain added protection by professional indemnity or similar forms of insurance. Your insurance broker should be able to advise whether this applies to your business.

CHAPTER 20

What to Charge

Prices sometimes cause new entrepreneurs a lot of agonizing. Even if you have worked in the trade before, you may not have been involved in deciding prices – or even thought much about it. Knowing material prices and the man-hours needed to make something, you may have started out, convinced that you could undercut existing businesses and still make a fat profit. However, as you read through the chapters of this book, you begin to appreciate other cost factors which have to be added to basic labour and material to arrive at total costs.

Perhaps there is not as much elbow room as you thought? If you cut prices to attract customers, you may pitch them so low that increasing turnover simply increases losses. John Bloom wasn't the first to discover this. On the other hand, if you don't sell cheaper than anyone else, how do you attract customers to a new business? The purpose of this chapter is to provide some understanding of what is involved in setting prices, to help you find the right price for *your* product or service.

Price, cost and value

The above three words are often used interchangeably in conversation. Their meanings are not identical, however. and to ensure clear thinking on the subject of prices, it is essential to appreciate their differences.

Price is the amount of money which is paid when something is bought or sold or when a service is provided. An article may have more than one price (e.g. a cash price and a credit price) and, as we all know, the same article may have different prices in different shops. Nevertheless, the price involved in a specific transaction is usually known precisely and is the same for both buyer and seller.

Cost is the amount of money which must be paid to obtain something. Cost may be the same as price but often is not. For instance, if you buy a piece of equipment, you may pay a certain price (£P). But before you can use it, you have to spend more, e.g. to have it delivered (£D) and installed (£I). Although its price is £P, its cost is £(P + D + I). This shows how costs can be additive, i.e. the installed cost is the sum of the price plus delivery cost plus the installation cost.

As explained in Chapter 12, there are many different kinds of cost: total cost, marginal cost, direct cost, out-of-pocket cost, and so on. The purpose for which a cost is to be used determines the correct cost to use. And even this 'correct' figure may be subject to uncertainty. Some cost items require judgement and allocation, into which an arbitrary element may intrude. In many cases, therefore, one cannot speak of an article as having a definite cost in the way one can speak of its having a definite price.

Value is what something is worth to someone and an article can be valued in three distinct ways.

Replacement value is what it will cost to replace. If it is readily available at the same price as you paid and does not involve additional costs for delivery and installation, its replacement value is the same as you paid for it. But replacement value, particularly in inflationary times, is often greater than the original price. Conversely, if the price of something is dropping rapidly (e.g. pocket calculators) its replacement value may be lower than its original price.

Sales value is what someone is willing to pay for something. This may be different from replacement value, as in the case of a piece of installed equipment. For a standard article in regular demand, the selling price may be easy to assess. For a non-standard article with an irregular demand, the selling price can be hard to predict, as auction realizations often show. Even if the selling price is known, some deduction must usually be made for selling expenses (e.g. advertising, sales salaries, commission, delivery) to arrive at the sales value.

Utility value is what something is worth under a particular set of circumstances. A car fuse costs only a few pence when you buy a spare at a garage. But when your car breaks down on a motorway on a winter night, its utility value may be very different. Then it will probably cost you several pounds to get a message through to a garage and persuade someone to drive out and deliver a fuse.

At this stage you may be wondering where *book value* comes in, i.e. the value of an item in your accounts. Book value is the result of applying accounting conventions to prices paid in the past. It is not related to market prices today and if it is the same as one of the above values it is an accident. Book value allows you to calculate the tax consequences of a price decision but it does not tell you what the price ought to be.

Mark-up or market?

There is a wide-spread belief that businessmen decide prices by calculating the cost and adding a 'mark-up' to provide a profit. This is rarely true. In practice, most businesses encounter a greater or lesser degree of competition. Regardless of what your costs may be, if you set prices too high, customers will 'vote with their feet' and buy from a competitor. Even in the unusual case of a unique product or service, you still have to decide what mark-up to apply. Virtually every product or service has an upper limit to price. Above this level, demand drops off because people cannot afford it or, even if they can, decide it is too dear. In short, prices are decided by the market, not by your costs.

When large and successful companies contemplate introducing a new product, they don't start by working out what it will cost. They start by deciding what they can sell it for and how much they can sell at that price. Then they work out how much it will cost to make that quantity and, by difference, see how much profit that will produce. In other words, the use of cost calculations is not to decide what price to charge – it is to decide whether the business is worth starting.

If your business provides something which is already available, it is not too hard to find out what the present market prices are by studying the shops, press advertising and sales catalogues. Then you must find out from suppliers what it will cost to buy the amount of goods you plan to sell. Adding on the other business expenses (e.g. rent, rates, salaries, interest, depreciation, etc.) and allowing for stock wastage and loss, you can work out the profit at that volume of business. Is it enough to make the project worth while?

You probably don't need to do this in a lot of detail, since the profit margin is much the same within a given class of goods. Some businesses, however, deal in several classes of goods; for instance a newsagent will usually sell confectionery and cigarettes as well as newspapers, each of which has a different profit margin. In such a case, you have to decide on a 'product mix', i.e. the proportion of each class of goods in the total. By far the best guide is personal experience in the trade; next best is advice from someone at present in the trade. You may get some idea by assessing how much space is devoted to each class in existing shops but this can be misleading, since the rate of stock turnover may differ for each class of goods.

In the case of services, the most common method of pricing is to charge on an hourly basis. This is sometimes supplemented by charging for travelling time, mileage or emergency callout. You may also impose a minimum charge to discourage very small jobs. If you cannot obtain information on current rates for your type of service, you may get some guidance from those for roughly comparable services, e.g. garage repairs, TV servicing, typing bureaux, etc.

Price cutting

Even when you know what the market price is for your goods or service, you may decide not to charge the same as your competitors. This will depend to a large extent on your business strategy, whether you are aiming for the low-price or the high-quality end of the market or steering a middle course. Unless you are deliberately aiming for the low-price end of the market, it is usually wise not to try to undercut your competitors but to compete in some other way such as quality, reliability or more effective promotion.

It is not enough just to cut prices and then wait passively for customers to flock to your door. The new business needs to be promoted actively in some way (see Chapter 17). But you are not earning money during the time you spend on promotion and whatever methods you use cost money. If you miscalculate, you may be caught on both sides of the profit equation – reduced income and increased expenditure. The danger is that you may fall into a vicious spiral of not earning enough to spend on promotion, thus failing to achieve the rapid growth which is essential at the beginning. Cutting prices may accentuate this process.

Your competitors are usually better established and have more resources than you. If you cut prices in an effort to win over some of their customers, they will probably cut theirs in retaliation. All they need do is match your efforts and sweat it out, hopefully recovering their losses by increasing their prices again – after you have gone bust! The winner of a price war is usually the one with the longest purse.

The beginner almost invariably underestimates some items of expenditure and, through inexperience, overlooks some entirely. As a result, he thinks he has more scope to cut prices than in fact exists. From analysis of costs into 'direct' and 'indirect', he persuades himself that, as long as he charges more than the direct costs for an 'extra' job, he is winning.

This is an insidious line of reasoning. If you reduce prices to one customer, the news gets around and it is hard to resist pressure from another customer to reduce prices to him – perhaps even retrospectively. One can easily slide into the position of doing so many 'extra' jobs at reduced margins that there are not enough 'basic' jobs to cover the indirect costs.

Another trap, which is particularly common in service businesses, is to overestimate the number of 'chargeable' hours, i.e. time spent on jobs which can be charged to a customer. You may not appreciate how much time you must spend during working hours talking to representatives, telephoning to locate supplies or picking up urgently needed goods from suppliers. Shoestring stock levels render new businesses particularly prone to this. Or you fall behind with your book-keeping and have to take time off 'work' to make up the wages or send out invoices or complete VAT returns.

Just think of the number of times when you came home from work, as an employee, and said, 'I've been all day at work and have nothing to show for it.' This can happen in your own business too. Such 'non-chargeable' time is a form of overhead, since it represents a loss of earnings. If you divide total expenditure by too high a figure for chargeable hours, you get too low an estimate for hourly costs.

Making a bid

As a contractor or sub-contractor, your customer is often not the general public but some other business or public sector organization. Many of the general principles of attracting customers still apply but there is one significant difference. Your customer – not you – decides what you will make or do. You have to make a bid for whatever the customer wants. Methods of preparing quotations for specific jobs are outside the scope of this book. This is a skill you must acquire as part of the preparation for starting your business. There are, however, some general points which apply to most bids.

Make adequate allowance, in both time and money, for the unforeseen. Materials or components may be damaged or defective on arrival, causing delay or incurring cost to rectify them. Strikes at the workplace of third parties can hold up supplies or delay your product delivery. You may need a clause in your contract to protect you against the effect of strikes.

Unless the job will be completed within a short time, you should try to include in the contract some clause to protect you against inflation. This may be in the form of an adjustment for any rise in price of specified materials or wages which occurs during the life of the contract. Alternatively, the contract price may be escalated in step with some agreed index, such as the Retail Price Index or Index of Average Earnings.

You must also try to safeguard your cash flow. If materials form a large part of the total job cost, try to persuade the customer to supply these. If purchased by you, ask for an appropriate part of the total bill to be paid promptly on production of supplier's invoices. Another way is to ask for payment to be phased, with perhaps one-quarter or one-third payable on signing the contract and one or more interim payments, leaving only 20–30 per cent remaining to be paid on completion.

For obvious reasons, few customers volunteer the information that they are willing to accept such terms, although many do if requested. You have little to lose by asking, since this is interpreted as business shrewdness – not financial weakness. You have much to lose by not asking, since your profit margin can be wiped out by inflation or interest charges. If the customer refuses, you must reconsider whether you want to bid for the job. If you do, it may be prudent to include something in the price for inflation and interest charges, although not necessarily named as such.

Discount for early payment

In previous chapters we have discussed the question of discounts for early payment from the buyer's viewpoint. Now we need to look at it from the other side of the counter. Is it a good idea to offer discounts? How much should you offer and how much will it cost you?

In answering these questions, the starting point is the custom in your trade. Practices vary greatly from one trade to another and it is usually best to follow normal trade practice. There are exceptions, however, since practices may have become established under conditions very different from those of today. It is worth considering, therefore, the advantages and disadvantages of deviating from custom.

Let us consider the case of Martin, in whose trade it is customary to offer $2\frac{1}{2}$ per cent discount for payment within 14 days. Does he gain or lose when a customer takes advantage of this? From his records he finds that, on average, accounts are paid 2 months after delivery of goods. The interest rate of his overdraft had fluctuated widely in recent years but at the time of making the study it was 18 per cent, equivalent to $1\frac{1}{2}$ per cent per month. By reducing the time lag between delivery and payment from two months to 14 days, Martin would save $1\frac{1}{2}$ months' interest at $1\frac{1}{2}$ per cent, making a total of $2\frac{1}{4}$ per cent. In short, by sacrificing $2\frac{1}{2}$ per cent on selling price he would save $2\frac{1}{4}$ per cent on interest, a net loss of $\frac{1}{4}$ per cent.

You can repeat the above calculations with your own figures to find out what your position would be. But your decision should not be made automatically on the result of the calculation. Interest rates vary considerably but you cannot switch discount policies on and off like a tap, every time the bank rate changes. It might be better to use an average interest rate over the past two or three years or, alternatively, your guess as to what it might be over the next few years.

In most businesses, interest rate is not the only consideration. There is usually a limit on overdrafts and once this is reached, the bank may be unwilling to raise it. Indeed, during periodic 'credit squeezes', banks sometimes reduce limits which were previously in force. Under these circumstances, additional working capital might be worth more than the current interest rate. If business is booming and you can earn 30–40 per cent on any additional capital you can find, Martin's discount terms would seem a bargain.

On the other hand, some businesses are not short of capital. They can afford to give generous credit terms, adjusting prices if necessary to ensure they do not lose on the deal. Such businesses may adopt a deliberate strategy of exploiting this sector of the market, i.e. those who need time to pay. Giving discounts for prompt payment would not fit such a strategy, regardless of normal trade practices.

CHAPTER 21

Building a Better Business

Few people who start a business expect it to stay at the original size for ever. Some just start and hope for the best but the wiser ones think about how they want it to grow before they start. In this way they hope to avoid doing something – or *not* doing something – which will make life difficult later on when the business grows.

The problems of success are less bitter than the problems of failure but they are still problems. Let's listen to what a number of entrepreneurs have to say about the snags they ran into when their business began to grow.

Joe runs a small chemical manufacturing business:

I was jogging along nicely when I got the chance of a big contract for making own brand household products for a supermarket chain. I borrowed the money to install new equipment on the strength of the contract. Then my troubles began. One or two early deliveries weren't up to scratch and had to be scrapped. Now the customer won't pay until after his lab has tested each batch – and they're slow. Then I had a fire in the stores and, because I hadn't increased my cover, the insurance company is arguing about paying. My supplier is getting difficult and demands cash on delivery. It's a struggle to raise the cash for wages some weeks and yet I'm making a good profit – on paper.

Sandra runs a boutique:

When I bought my shop, a small upstairs flat went with it. I moved in there to live, which helped to keep expenses down in the beginning. I seem to have a flair for buying the right things for they sell like hot cakes. In fact I could sell twice as much if I had a bigger shop. The simple answer was to expand the shop into the flat above, so I found somewhere else to live. Imagine the shock when the local council stopped me from doing what they called 'converting a dwelling house into commercial premises'.

Mary has a typing bureau:

When my husband died, the small pension wasn't enough to keep the children. I had been a good secretary before I married so I started this bureau because I could run it from home. It was uphill work but after two years I had another girl, Elaine, working for me full-time. Then I started to get work from Adpost Ltd, a local mail-order firm. They paid well – and promptly – expanded rapidly and soon were our biggest customer. When Elaine's husband was transferred, she left and I had to drop all the other customers and work long hours myself to keep on top of the Adpost work. Then came the bombshell. Adpost were taken over and the new manager just told me one Friday that there would be no more work for me – they had decided to transfer it to their main office. I had to start from the bottom all over again.

Harold runs an antique clock shop in partnership with his wife Betty:

When I was made redundant at 52, I decided to abandon my old career and exploit my hobby – repairing antique clocks. We opened a shop in our village which is in a popular tourist area. As a sideline, Betty began to attend auctions and buy up broken clocks which I repaired and sold. We became known in the trade and are now flooded with work. Or should I say we were – until we took so long to do repairs that we began to lose customers. It has stabilized now but we could easily get much more work than I can handle.

Limits to growth

There is much talk these days about limits to growth encountered in society, e.g. food, energy, social organization. There is debate about whether these limits really exist and, if they do, how they might be overcome. There is little doubt that limits do exist to the growth of businesses. Fortunately, methods are available for overcoming most of these limits.

These limits to growth, some of which are illustrated by the experiences described above, include:
- lack of time to look for new work, train staff, improve working methods and organize the business;
- lack of money for building up stocks, buying new equipment and promoting the business;
- lack of space for running the business, holding stocks, installing equipment and trying out new developments;
- lack of trained staff;
- over-dependence on a single customer;
- the ability of the owner and/or staff to adjust to changing circumstances.

To some extent these difficulties arise through a wrong balance of resources between the *operation* and the *development* of the business. By operation is meant those activities required for the day-to-day running of the business, e.g. getting supplies, fulfilling orders, managing staff and routine administration. By development is meant those activities designed to increase business in the future, e.g. developing new products, finding new customers, training staff and improving working methods.

It is obvious that operation is mainly concerned with *today* and development with *tomorrow*. If you don't pay enough attention to today, there won't be a tomorrow. If you don't pay enough attention to tomorrow, you will fail to adapt as circumstances change and one day there won't be a today.

To some extent also, these difficulties arise through the twin penalties of success – overwork and overtrading.

Overwork is a signal that *time resources* are under stress. Some of us can work for much longer hours than others but we all have a limit. Once that limit is exceeded, certain well-recognized symptoms appear. The individual has more difficulty in dealing with other people. He becomes more impulsive and finds it harder to think clearly. He makes more wrong decisions or else refuses to make decisions. He gets very touchy if anyone points out his mistakes or pesters him for a decision. If the stress continues for long, he may have a sudden breakdown.

Overtrading is a signal that *cash resources* are under stress. Most businesses follow the basic cash-flow cycle: (1) money paid for supplies, (2) money paid to staff to convert supplies into product, (3) money received when the product is sold. There are time lags at each stage and working capital is needed to cope with these lags and any fluctuations in them.

When a business is expanding, the amounts paid out each time stages (1) and (2) come round are higher than in the previous cycle. But there is a delay before the higher income is received at stage (3). If the working capital is not increased proportionately, there is less 'slack' to cope with fluctuations. The business becomes more vulnerable and, if the unforeseen arises, it can go bust through lack of cash even though, on paper, it is making a profit.

Development of a business thus calls for extra work and extra capital, in addition to that needed for operating the business. The need to avoid overwork and overtrading, therefore, sets limits to the *rate of growth* of the business.

Development strategy

The best way to keep a proper balance between the resources allocated to operating and development and to avoid the perils of overwork and overtrading is to have a development strategy. This may sound a rather grandiose thing for a small business but it is not a luxury. Many of the problems described at the beginning of this chapter could have been avoided with a bit of forethought. Making a development strategy is a form of mental discipline which ensures that you think through your problems in advance and thus avoid or at least be prepared for them.

To be successful in building up a business, you must have a strong opportunistic streak. You must be able to spot new opportunities for expanding your existing business and for branching out into related activities. This means that you need to have a clear picture of what your existing business *is* and the ability to assess how well new ideas will fit in with it.

If you don't have a clear picture, the tendency is to look at each new idea as a fresh venture, instead of studying it in the light of your existing business. This can waste much time and mental effort. One of the main purposes of a development strategy is to help you in the appraisal of new ideas.

Management textbooks often criticize how large companies and even whole industries have declined through an over-narrow development strategy. You read of how film companies failed through thinking they were in the film business instead of the entertainment business. How transatlantic liner companies died through thinking they were in shipping instead of in passenger transportation.

The moral of this is not that you have to think big to be successful but that your development strategy should be in proportion to your present scale of operation. A company with a large share of a static or declining industry *needs* to move into another industry to give it scope for development. Hence the present efforts of the major tobacco companies to establish themselves in other industries. But a new business usually has such a small share of the market that there is plenty of room for growth within the same industry.

Let us hear how Sid plans to develop his business:

I'm halfway through my first year running my own grocery shop. I've used my previous experience as a manager to set up a Five-Year Development Plan:

Year 1 – survive and learn the business;
Year 2 – push up sales 50 per cent and double profits to provide money for expansion;
Year 3 – buy a second grocery shop a few miles away which I'll run while my chief assistant takes over this shop;
Year 4 – repeat the exercise of expanding business in the new shop and train up another shop manager;
Year 5 – open up a third shop, twice the size of this one.

Because I know *what* I plan to do, I can measure my progress towards it. Because I know *when* I want to do things, I know the right time to start preparations for them – not too soon and not too late.

The first point to notice about his story is that Sid's strategy is clear – to build up a chain of grocery shops. The second point is that he is allowing himself time to gain experience: of the grocery trade, of training staff, of buying new premises, of running several shops. He is not trying to take too many new steps at once. Finally, his plan is in sufficient detail to provide a scale of both money and time but is also sufficiently flexible so that he can slow down or speed up in the light of events.

Allocating resources

In Chapters 13, 14 and 15, I discussed control – control of the business, control of money and control of time. Sid has set up his Development Plan in a way which makes it easy to control all three of these, both in the operation of the existing business and its development. This is critical. A Development Strategy is just a dream until you prepare a Development Plan to show how you will translate it into action. Similarly, a plan is just a pious hope until you set up controls to check how it is working out in practice.

Your controls should tell you, in particular, how you are dividing your resources between *operation* and *development*. To keep your accounts simple, it is best to charge all expenditure to the business as a whole. Don't try to keep two sets of books, one for operation and one for development. The number of cost items which can be attributed to development is usually only a small proportion of the total. It is therefore not too much trouble to keep a separate note of how much you spend each month on development.

In allocating time, you must distinguish between time of paid staff and your own time. Time spent on development by staff can easily be converted into money, based on salary costs, and added to the other development expenditure. Total development expenditure can then be expressed as a percentage of total business expenditure. The time spent by yourself on development should, however, be kept in time units and expressed as a percentage of the total time you spend each month on the business.

You now have two simple measures of the resources devoted to development each month – money and your own time – each expressed as a percentage of total resources employed. What should these figures be?

There is, alas, no magic ratio to which all businesses should conform. It will be affected, obviously, by what you can afford. If you can afford very little, your business will grow only slowly. In this case you might ask yourself if, how and when you should raise some money specifically for development. (Incidentally, presentation of a well-thought-out development strategy, development plan and control system will be of great help in persuading people to lend you money.)

Alternatively, good fortune may sometimes provide more cash than you need immediately for either operation or your existing development plan. It is tempting to look around, almost wildly, for some new idea. Don't. Put the money in a secure but easily accessible investment (e.g. a building society share account) until you have a good reason to use it.

In general, however, new businesses tend to find resources scarce rather than plentiful and cash and your own time are often the limitations on growth. In such circumstances, the best policy is usually to favour development as much as you dare, without causing serious trouble in operation. Remember too that money and time are to some extent convertible by hiring or not hiring outside help. Use this conversion when necessary to keep resources in balance.

Developing ideas

Some people seem to bubble over with ideas, to be able to keep producing them effortlessly. Some of their ideas may be a bit crazy but they produce so many that a fair number turn out pretty good. Often someone else takes them up and sometimes makes a lot of money out of them. Ever wondered why the idea creators themselves rarely profit from them?

It is chiefly a matter of temperament. The personal qualities needed to produce ideas are very different from those needed to assess ideas and put them into practice. The ideas man gets his fun from *generating* ideas. He feels exhilarated by the flow of inspiration. He becomes inhibited if he has to judge them good or bad because it stops the flow. He lacks the patience for the rather dull slogging which is often needed to turn ideas into reality.

Some people can switch from one role to another,

depending on their mood, and if you can produce your own ideas that is fine. But if you can't, don't worry because other people will supply them. What is indispensable, however, is the ability to judge ideas and spot the good ones. In fact, it may be easier to deal with other people's ideas – it's not so difficult to discard the bad ones.

Your Development Strategy is a great help in judging ideas. Ask yourself if this idea fits in with the mainstream of your strategy. If it doesn't, be careful. Ask yourself if it is closely related to your mainstream business. Does it use skills that you or your staff already possess? Is it something your present customers will be interested in? Can you handle it through your present shop or workplace? Can it be promoted through your existing sales outlets? Unless the answer is 'yes' to most of these questions, it is probably not a good idea *for you*.

If the idea fits in well with your strategy, study how it can be built into your Development Plan. What will have to be abandoned or postponed to cope with the new effort? What will the effect of this be? Is it worth it? If you need additional resources, where will you get them and what will they cost you? If the new idea turns out a flop, will it destroy your existing business?

Developing the organization

A large company needs a fairly formal type of organization so that everyone knows what they are expected to do and how they should do it. This is not needed in the early days of a small business when so many problems are being met for the first time because the boss is usually on the spot to give quick decisions.

The great strength of many a new business is the high ratio of brain power to muscle power. The whole point of developing your business is, however, to make it a bigger business and, as the number of employees increases, it is important to try to counteract the dilution of this ratio. You must, therefore, continually adapt your organization to meet changing needs as the business grows.

Many people think of an organization chart as the symbol of 'big business' rigidity. It need not be so. The important thing about a chart is that it shows who is responsible for what and to whom. In a small business the same individual's name can appear on the chart in several different places as responsible for different activities.

As a small business grows, so does the staff, and new names appear on the chart. The owner can begin to delegate responsibility for 'production' or 'sales' or 'administration' to assistants who have proved their worth. The important thing is to revise the chart when this happens so that it always shows an up-to-date picture. An equally important thing is to create such an atmosphere that, although responsibility may be assigned to one person, other staff are willing to help him if they have the time and ability to do so.

As experience is gained, you will find that a number of jobs seem to crop up frequently. When you spot this, it is time to think about how these jobs are done. Analyse the present methods, discuss them with the people who do the jobs and, if necessary, get expert advice from outside. Based on this study, work out the best way of doing the job.

Write down the method and begin to build up a catalogue of standard methods to which anyone given a job can refer. From time to time discuss the jobs in this catalogue with the staff concerned to see if methods can be improved – if necessary by installing new equipment. Can the cost of this new equipment be justified and, if installed, could you use it for other jobs?

To get the best utilization of manpower – and to cover for sickness and holidays – it is desirable for each member of your staff to be able to do several different jobs. In theory, there should be at least two people able to do each job and at least one person able to stand in for you on a short-term basis.

The catalogue of standard methods is a step in this direction but it may also be necessary to train some staff to develop their skills. If this can be done at little out-of-pocket cost and during slack business periods, you should not hesitate. Where it is necessary to send the individual on an outside training course, which may be expensive, you must think harder. You should consider the cost of the training, how you can cope in his absence, the enhanced value of the individual after training and the likelihood of his staying with you long enough for you to get the benefit.

One of the big problems in developing the small organization is the 'step' problem. To increase total staff from two to three is an increase of 50 per cent. One can rarely increase the volume of business suddenly by this amount and therefore special measures should be taken to reduce the size of the step. Before engaging the third person, the effective workforce should be increased to as near three as possible by such means as: overtime, temporary staff, sub-contracting, outworkers, etc. Needless to say, these extra measures should be cut back sharply as soon as the additional staff member starts work.

CHAPTER 22

Dreams and Reality

Having read through the book so far, the choice is yours. Do you really want to start your own business? If your answer is NO, the book has probably saved you a lot of money and heartache. Perhaps you are uncertain. You may have a secure, well-paid job which provides most of what you want in life. In the meantime you like to think of being your own boss ... one day. Well, maybe you had better carry on dreaming.

Perhaps you feel that you certainly do want to start your own business but you lack something specific – money, experience, or whatever. Then I suggest that you begin to prepare yourself for an entrepreneurial career, but don't burn your boats until you feel you are ready. To start a business without self-confidence is asking for trouble. But that is no reason for wasting time – get busy overcoming whatever is lacking.

If your answer is a clear YES, then read on. The purpose of this chapter is to give you the best possible chance of success in starting your business. We shall go step by step along the path that leads from dreams to reality.

Step 1: Set your objectives

The importance of motivation is discussed in Chapter 1, where I make the point that many entrepreneurs seek more than money in starting a business. This is examined in more detail in Chapter 3. Does this apply to you? The first step towards reality is to get very clear in your mind what kind of reality you want.

How much money do you expect to make in terms of both

income and capital accumulation? How hard are you prepared to work to achieve this? What kind of work are you willing to do and what kind do you prefer? How much are you prepared to sacrifice in terms of family life, leisure, holidays, standard of living – and for how long? How much contact with others do you seek?

Having got your objectives clear in your mind, write them down. The need to find the right words to express yourself on paper is an excellent discipline. It helps to cut out the mental 'arm-waving' and forces you to be clear and concise. Chapter 3 shows the points which should be considered.

Step 2: Outline your business

Write down a brief outline of your proposed business. What is your major activity – making, selling or providing a service? What is your main product or service? What is your class of market – luxury, economy or middle of the road? Who are your customers – individual members of the public or organizations in the public or private sectors? These questions have all been discussed at length in previous chapters and you have probably made up your mind by now. If not, you must settle these points before going any further.

Now look at the business objectives you have written down and compare them with your outline. Take them one by one and ask yourself whether this business will enable you to meet that objective. Be as honest as you can in answering 'yes', 'no', or 'maybe'. One cannot expect perfection and so you may find you have answered 'maybe' in some cases; perhaps there is even a 'no'.

If you have answered 'no', you must re-examine that particular objective. Is it essential or only desirable? Are there other ways of achieving it, outside your business? Does your proposed business make it impossible to meet that objective? Can the business be modified in some way to enable you to meet it? (At this stage your business exists only on paper, so it is easy to change.) Repeat the process with the objectives to which you have answered 'maybe'.

You may have to go through several trial-and-error attempts before you achieve a set of objectives, which represents what you really want to achieve, and a business outline which offers a reasonable prospect of achieving them.

Step 3: Prepare yourself

Having achieved a satisfactory match between objectives and outline, the latter must now be compared with your own strengths and weaknesses. In Chapter 2, the needs of various businesses are discussed in terms of skills, knowledge, experience, resources, etc. Using this chapter to jog your memory, write down a list of those required by the business you have chosen. Refer now to the answers you wrote down to the self-assessment questions in Chapter 1. Using these as a guide, write down a brief comment on the extent to which you meet – or fail to meet – each business requirement.

How are you going to cope with those needs which are not properly covered? You may be able to make some of these 'needs' superfluous by altering the business outline. You may be able to get someone else to do what you cannot, e.g. by taking a partner who is strong where you are weak, engaging staff with appropriate skills or contracting-out some of the work.

Sometimes the problem cannot be solved in this way. You may not know of a suitable partner or the business may not be able to afford staff in the beginning. In any case, it is unwise to be too dependent on others for some kinds of knowledge, for instance basic experience of the trade in which your business will operate. It will greatly enhance your chances of success if you remedy this serious weakness before you start your business – even if it means some delay.

In some trades, training courses for beginners are provided by government agencies, trade associations, industry training boards or suppliers. You might also try to get a part-time job working for someone in the trade. While this is going on, you can fill up other gaps in your knowledge by reading (see Appendix 1), evening classes or correspondence courses. You should also be trying to increase your store of capital.

Step 4: Form your strategy

Each of the first three steps represents progress along the path from your dream to reality. This fourth step is probably the greatest of all, since it takes you into the nitty-gritty of how you are going to run the business you have chosen. Essential though they are, words like 'objective' and 'outline' have a rather abstract flavour. Now at last you can feel you are 'getting down to business' in every sense of the term.

In Chapter 7, I described how I used my 'thinkbooks' to develop the habit of constructive thinking. If you have not already done so, I suggest you begin your 'thinkbooks' now. Start it the way I did, with one loose-leaf binder and some card dividers to keep the sections in order. As the book grows, you can hive off sections into new binders when it becomes necessary. What you jot down now will provide your first entries under 'Strategy'.

Let me explain what I mean by 'business strategy'. The Concise Oxford Dictionary defines 'strategy' as 'management of an army or armies in a campaign, art of so moving or disposing troops or ships or aircraft as to impose upon the enemy the place and time and conditions for fighting preferred by oneself'.

In the business scene, a strategy provides a means of getting greater control of events, so that they happen in a way which helps you to achieve your objectives. Is this not better than just being carried along, continually surprised by what happens and not knowing how to react when it does?

It is of course not enough to have any old strategy. It must be a good one, well suited to your circumstances. This implies that you know what your objectives are (Step 1), that you have chosen your 'battlefield' (Step 2) and that you have prepared yourself for the campaign ahead (Step 3). Having got this far, how now do you prepare a strategy?

When facing a complex task, it is usually helpful to break it down into smaller and more 'handleable' bits. Then you don't have to think of so many different things at once and you can tackle the more urgent bits first. There is no ideal way of sub-dividing a business strategy which suits every case but the example of Fred, given below, shows a fairly typical pattern of breakdown which would fit many businesses.

Fred's objectives were: (1) independence, (2) variety of work and (3) an income of £10,000 a year after ploughing back some of the profits to expand the business. He intended to achieve these by starting a business as a welding contractor. This is how he described his strategy:

Operation – Establish a small workshop where I shall carry out short-run, high-quality, sub-contract jobs.

Organization – Start as a sole trader with a registered business name. Act as salesman and welder myself while my wife keeps the books and handles the office work.

Customers – Mainly engineering firms. Circularize firms within a 25-mile radius and visit likely prospects.

Workplace – Rent a workshop within a 10-mile radius of home. I need about 1,000 sq. ft with good ventilation, 3-phase power supply, telephone, lorry access and some outside storage space.

Equipment and supplies – Need two welding machines

and stocks of gas, welding rods, tools, etc. Also a van for collection and delivery.

Staff – Start off on my own, supplemented by some of my mates at evenings and weekends when necessary. Will hire a good welder, as soon as workload justifies it, and pay him 10 per cent above local factory rates.

Money – Need about £3,000 fixed capital, comprising welding machines and accessories (£2,000) and a second-hand van (£1,000). Need about £2,500 working capital, based on material float (£1,000) and three months' running expenses at £120 per week (rent, rates, electricity, petrol, etc. and £50 'drawings' for myself). I have about £1,000 in savings and can perhaps re-mortgage my house.

Information – Need to find out about VAT, tax, PAYE and NHI, contracts, employment and safety laws. Need to find an accountant and solicitor. Need to arrange part-time engineering consultant, draughtsman and maintenance mechanic from work acquaintances.

So there you have Fred's strategy in a nutshell. He was now ready to get under way.

Step 5: Go into action

The general principles of preparing an action plan are discussed in Chapter 7 and therefore need not be repeated here. The application of these is illustrated by continuing the story of Fred. He decided that, for the first stage of his plan, he would concentrate his efforts on four strategy headings (Workplace, Equipment and supplies, Money, Information), leaving the other four until later.

Under 'Workplace' he had one action item – *Contact local authorities* – so he telephoned the offices of the three district councils whose areas came within a 10-mile radius.

To his dismay, he discovered that none had any workshops to rent, nor did they know of any likely to become vacant in the near future. They did, however, suggest a few private landlords he might contact. They also reminded him that it was unlawful to run a welding business at a location not covered by appropriate planning permission.

Under 'Equipment and supplies' he also had one action item, viz. *Enquire about welding equipment*. From his welding experience, it was easy to draw up a detailed list of the equipment he needed. With the help of his firm's purchasing officer and a few telephone calls, he obtained quotations for these. Not surprisingly these days, prices were a little higher than he expected. He also found that there was a 3-month delivery time on welding machines but that most of the other equipment could be obtained within a few days.

Under 'Money' he had two items. The first, *Talk to bank manager*, was disappointing but not unfruitful. His bank manager was willing to grant an overdraft of up to £1,000 and might increase this as he built up a good track record. The bank was not prepared to grant a loan for purchase of equipment, but suggested that a subsidiary company might be prepared to lease the welding machines to Fred.

Fred talked to his building society about the second item – *Enquire about remortgaging house*. They were undergoing one of their periodic squeezes, however, and were unable to help. They suggested he might approach his insurance company. The latter was willing to give a 5-year loan of £4,000 on the security of a second mortgage – at 15 per cent interest!

Under 'Information' he had three items – *Appoint accountant*, *Appoint solicitor* and *Fix part-time specialists*. The first two he did on recommendations from his bank manager. The talk with his accountant was particularly helpful. The accountant suggested that he was trying to start on too grand a scale and, instead of borrowing £4,000, he should try to scale down his capital needs. For instance, why not buy only one welding machine and delay the second until an assistant was hired? Why not buy the van on HP?

He also asked Fred if he could start on a part-time basis. Although this would reduce his income at first, he would be able to contribute to the business from his normal earnings, instead of withdrawing money from the business. The accountant also explained to Fred the tax advantages of not having a high profit in the first year.

The maintenance mechanic he fixed up suggested that Fred might buy a second-hand welding machine, costing half the price of a new one, and offered to help Fred inspect and overhaul one. He also proposed that, instead of buying a van, Fred could get a car-trailer and simply hire a van by the day when a big job cropped up.

Step 6: Watch your progress

On completing this first stage, Fred sat back and reviewed the progress he had made. He could see that finding a workplace would not be easy and he might have to extend the 10-mile limit. In any event, this was now a high priority item. Regarding equipment, he had a number of alternatives to study for obtaining the welding machine (he had already reduced this to one) and the van or trailer.

Since no decision could be made about money until the equipment studies were completed, they were urgent. So too was consideration of starting on a part-time basis. He had now learned about cash-flow calculations, which would be useful in making these decisions. It seemed that, under certain conditions, he might be able to start the business within the resources of his £1,000 savings for fixed capital and the £1,000 overdraft for working capital. This would leave the remortgage potential of his house available to finance expansion at a later stage when, perhaps, interest rates might be more favourable.

Fred now decided to set up a regular routine of planning

his actions a month at a time, with a review at the month-end before making his next action plan. During the coming month, he plans to take a few days' 'holiday' and spend them exploring the district thoroughly, looking for a work-place. During his travels he will also knock on a few doors and try to get some future customers lined up.

Over to you

We shall take leave of Fred while he is still in the midst of translating his dreams into reality. At the time of writing, he has reached 'reality' in a form not too different from that originally planned. He has not yet achieved all his objectives but is still travelling hopefully – and happily – towards them.

To be honest, you are probably much more interested in your own future than that of Fred. Are you going to follow his example and translate *your* dreams into reality? If you do, I hope you will find this book useful. I have enjoyed writing it – because it is the realization of one of my own dreams.

Good luck!

APPENDIX 1

Further Reading

There are literally thousands of books dealing with business. It is therefore impossible to present a list which even approaches completeness. Nor would it be helpful to try, since the founders of new businesses are usually busy people. I have deliberately kept the following list short and confined it to books which, I believe, will be useful to a large number of readers.

Some of these books contain bibliographies which may indicate further books worth reading for your particular business. Advice about books on particular topics can be obtained from the sources listed in Appendix 2.

How to pick up the right small business opportunity – Kenneth J. Albert (McGraw-Hill Book Company, 1977, 232pp) Detailed description of how to select a business which matches your abilities and objectives.

Be your own boss – Alan Fiber (Management Books, 1967, 158pp) General book for beginners, giving many ideas for business opportunities.

The complete guide to retail management – Alan Fiber (Penguin Books, 1972, 320pp) A readable book giving thorough coverage of the retail trade.

How to win customers – Heinz M. Goldman (Pan Management Series, 1971, 325pp) Excellent book on selling and salesmanship.

Working for yourself – Godfrey Golzen (Kogan Page, 1978, 230pp) The *Daily Telegraph* guide to self-employment; good general guide.

Mind your own business – H. J. W. Kay (Kay's Property Agents, 12pp) Presents, in a few pages, much useful information about buying a going concern.

Career change – Ruth Lancashire and Roger Holdsworth (CRAC, 1976, 108pp) Contains an excellent section on self-assessment.

Occupation self-employed – Rosemary Pettit (Wildwood House, 1981, 197pp) Describes experiences of 60 self-employed people in a wide range of businesses giving, in many cases, a rough indication of income.

Starting and running a small business – Alan Sproxton (United Writers Publications, 1977, 129pp) Light-hearted approach to starting a business, strong on mail-order selling.

Mind your own business – (Distributive Industry Training Board, 60pp) Very clear description of how to assess markets, decide upon stock policy and control costs in the retail trade.

Earning money at home – Ed. Edith Rudinger (Consumers Association, 1980, 192pp) Good exposition of what is involved in working at home; discussion of various home businesses.

The buyer's right – (Consumers Association and the Open University, 1978, 207pp) Clear account of the law as it affects the consumer: budgeting and borrowing, choosing goods and services, making the deal, what to do if things go wrong.

Tax-saving guide – (Consumers Association, 192pp – distributed free each year to subscribers to *Money Which*) In my opinion the best guide available on handling your income tax, including that from self-employment.

The following three books are published in conjunction with a monthly updating service by Croner Publications Ltd, Croner House, 173 Kingston Road, New Malden, Surrey KT3 3SS (tel: 01-942 8966):

Reference book for the self employed and smaller business – Describes in clear and concise terms the up-to-date rules and regulations of most interest to entrepreneurs: company law, taxation, VAT, national insurance, health and safety, employment and consumer laws.

Reference book for employers – Clearly written guide on the Acts of Parliament, EEC regulations and orders relating to the employment of persons in factories, offices, shops, etc.

Buying and selling law – Authoritative and practical guide to the law governing the supply of goods and services.

There is also a very good series of booklets published by the Small Firms Service of the Department of Trade and Industry. These booklets are simple, clearly written and free. They cover many topics of interest to anyone starting a business but, since the titles in print vary from time to time, I have not tried to list them below. Your best plan is to telephone the nearest centre (Freefone 2444) and obtain the booklets which best fit your needs.

The Small Firms Service has also just started (September 1983) a free bi-monthly newspaper, *In Business Now*, specifically geared to meet the needs of small and growing businesses. It gives news of changes in rules and regulations, small-business success stories, government-sponsored schemes, services available in various parts of the country, etc. You can obtain a specimen copy from the Small Firms Service or put yourself on the mailing list by writing to: In Business Now, Freepost, London SW1P 4BR.

Getting Help

The new entrepreneur needs help in many ways – information, advice, guidance, financial and other tangible forms of assistance. Contrary to popular belief, much help is available to those starting a business, far more indeed than there ever was in the past. Much of it, however, applies only to certain areas, to certain types of business and is sometimes 'on offer' for only a limited period of time. The inexperienced entrepreneur may sometimes encounter difficulty in finding out what help is available to him – and under what conditions – but it is usually a rewarding exercise.

A number of sources of help are listed below. It would be quite impossible to give a complete list since it would be much too long for this book. Moreover, new sources are continually springing up and, to a lesser extent, old ones dying. The following list should be regarded as illustrative of what is available in most parts of the country. If you cannot find what you seek in this list, use some of those listed as 'jumping-off' points to lead you to what you want.

Because the field is so wide and ever-changing, some of those trying to help you may not know the full picture themselves. You may therefore get contradictory or confusing advice. Try to be patient and tolerant. They mean well and most of them are extremely, almost overwhelmingly helpful. If you become confused, you just have to persist, trying other sources until you find one that can explain it all clearly.

The mention of a particular organization in the following list does not constitute a seal of approval; nor does omission from the list imply the opposite. Needs vary widely from one reader to another. Moreover, the policy, aims and effectiveness of an organization can change over a period of time. Readers are therefore strongly advised to investigate thoroughly, obtain professional advice when it seems appropriate and, in general, apply normal business prudence before entering into any commitments.

Libraries

These are the obvious starting points for many quests for information, not only for facts but also for tracking down other sources which can tell you what you want to know. If your local branch does not have a good reference section, they can tell you where the nearest one is. They can also obtain most books for you through the inter-library network.

If the reference library is distant, you may be able to find out what you want by telephone, or at least check that they have the right book in stock before you go there. Don't forget also that 'private' libraries belonging to educational, trade and professional bodies are usually willing to allow outsiders to consult books on their premises, even if you may not borrow them.

There are two reference books which readers may find particularly useful as information sources. *Directory of British Associations* (CBD Research Ltd) gives an extensive listing of trade associations, professional societies, research associations, etc. *U.K. Kompass* gives a comprehensive listing of businesses, arranged geographically with an alphabetical index, giving details of size, nature of business, name of chief executive, etc. This can be used to find suppliers, competitors and potential customers in your own district.

Citizens' Advice Bureau

This is another excellent starting point. You can find the address from your post office or telephone directory. They

have a wide fund of knowledge, and if they don't know the
answer to a question they can usually tell you who does.

Local authorities

These provide many forms of help to people starting a new
business including, in some cases, local grants as well as
government grants. They can advise you on how to meet
the requirements of the laws they administer, e.g.
consumer protection, planning permission, issue of certain
licences.

In addition, they are often substantial landlords of
business premises such as shops, offices and, in some areas,
factories. They may be able to help you find accommodation, perhaps at an attractive rent, and they sometimes
offer help in equipping premises and in hiring and training
initial staff.

Small Firms Service

This service, run by the Department of Trade and Industry,
operates through twelve regional Small Firms Centres. If
you ask the telephone operator for Freefone 2444 you will
be put through to the nearest centre. These provide a wide-
ranging information service to anyone running, or thinking
of starting, a small business. They can also tell you of other
services which are available in your particular district.

The information service is supplemented by a number of
area counselling offices, where clients can discuss their
business plans and problems with a counsellor. (These
latter are recently retired businessmen with experience in
small firms.) The first three counselling sessions are free,
after which there is a charge of £20 for each further session.

Council for Small Industries in Rural Areas (CoSIRA)

This government-sponsored organization provides advice and loans to help small manufacturing and service industries in rural areas. 'Small industries' are those normally employing not more than twenty skilled people and 'rural areas' include country towns of up to 10,000 inhabitants. Small tourist enterprises are eligible, but not agriculture, horticulture or retail trades (except for isolated village stores).

A preliminary talk, free and without obligation, can be arranged by contacting the local Organizer (see telephone directory under CoSIRA). After this, you will be told the charge for any further services required. CoSIRA also offers loans for buildings, plant, equipment and working capital in approved cases.

Enterprise Agencies

There are now about 160 enterprise agencies throughout the UK, ranging from one-man bands up to the London Enterprise Agency (Lenta) with a staff of 20. They are usually set up by local private companies getting together with local authorities, and provide a variety of services for new entrepreneurs: introductory courses on running a business, free counselling, help in finding premises, exhibitions, even cash grants in some cases. Check with your local authority whether there is an enterprise agency in your district and what it offers.

Chambers of Trade/Commerce

Most districts have a Chamber of Trade, a local organization consisting mainly of local retailers but also perhaps including representatives of department and multiple stores and other businesses operating in the district. Sometimes these are called Chambers of Commerce and in some districts both may be found. In the latter case, 'Trade' may be oriented towards retail business and 'Commerce' towards manufacturing but the division is not always clear.

These bodies organize social and trade events and liaise with local authorities on matters of common interest, e.g. parking facilities, shopping hours, town planning proposals, etc. Some also provide advice and services to members. These organizations are usually listed in the telephone directory or you can find out their addresses from local bank branches.

Trade Associations

These bodies usually provide a range of services to their members, sometimes including advice and training for new entrants to the trade. It is therefore worth finding out the cost of membership and the services offered by the one(s) appropriate to your business. Before deciding whether to join, it may be helpful to get an opinion on the association(s) from people already in the trade.

There are two trade associations of particular interest to small businesses:

(a) *National Federation of Self Employed and Small Businesses Ltd.* Formed in 1974, this organization now has nearly 50,000 members in over 300 branches. Full membership costs £18 per annum (plus £10 initial joining fee), which entitles members to a monthly newspaper, *First Voice*, a legal advisory service, and a legal protection scheme, all without further charge. If you are interested in joining, you can obtain a comprehensive, free 'Be Your Own Boss Pack' by writing to: 140 Lower Marsh, Westminster Bridge, London SE1 (tel: 01-928 9272).

(b) *Alliance of Small Firms and Self-Employed People Ltd (ASP).* Formed in 1975, ASP has no branch structure; instead its staff give immediate information and advice to members' queries, backed by experienced consultants for more complex problems. Membership costs £15 per annum, which entitles members to a free legal advisory service and a bi-monthly magazine, *Counterattack*. A legal insurance scheme is available for an additional £15 p.a.; members may also purchase a number of books and pamphlets. For further details write to: 42 Vine Road, East Molesey, Surrey KT8 9LF (tel: 01-979 2293).

Universities, polytechnics, colleges of further education

Staff of higher educational institutions are usually very pleased to help local industries. For enquiries which can be answered 'off the cuff' this is usually free, but if they have to spend some time on the job they are likely to charge you. You should clarify this at the outset.

Some institutions have an Industrial Liaison Officer (the title may differ) to whom enquiries should be made. In other cases, you might approach the Department of Management Studies or, with straightforward factual queries, the appropriate department.

An increasing number of institutions now provide courses for those thinking of starting or running small businesses. These range from one day to several weeks, from full-time day to part-time evening classes. They are often inexpensive and it may be worth enquiring of your nearest institution, who should be able to tell you not only what they run but also what is available elsewhere.

Government departments

A range of free folders and booklets, relevant to the needs of small businesses, is usually available at the local offices of government departments – Inland Revenue, DHSS, VAT, Jobcentres, Manpower Services Commission, etc. Officials are usually willing to discuss particular problems and, in some cases, can arrange visits of advisers to your business premises. If you don't know which department is responsible for a particular matter, the Small Firms Service should be able to tell you.

Banks

The clearing banks provide a variety of services through local branch managers or regional teams of specialists. These services (and their cost) differ from bank to bank and from time to time so it is necessary to find out from local branches what services are currently offered by your own and other banks and what they will charge you. You should not assume that your own bank will automatically give you the best deal or that the service they offer is the one best suited to your needs. Shop around and do your homework before deciding.

Under the Loan Guarantee Scheme set up in 1981, small businesses may be eligible for a loan guarantee for amounts up to £75,000, repayable over two to seven years. In suitable cases, the Department of Industry is prepared to guarantee 80 per cent of medium-term loans (not overdrafts) made by certain banks and financial institutions. The Department makes a charge for the guarantee (usually 3 per cent per annum of the sum guaranteed) and the interest rate for the loan is set by the lender. A leaflet describing the scheme is available from the Small Firms Service.

Suppliers

Suppliers of equipment, components and technical products sometimes assist customers with equipment-servicing and repair, technical advice on product application and trouble-shooting. Some also provide training for entrepreneurs and their staff. These services may be free or charged, so find out before you use them.

Voluntary buying groups

Readers will be aware of the existence of voluntary buying groups in certain retail tades, e.g. 'Spar' in groceries and 'Stermat' in ironmongery. Less well known is that some of these groups also provide services to their members, including training for new entrants to the trade.

Index

Health and self-help books now available in Panther Books

W H Bates		
Better Eyesight Without Glasses	£1.95	☐
Ronald Gatty		
The Body Clock Diet	£1.50	☐
Desmonde Dunne		
Yoga Made Easy	£1.95	☐
Laurence E Morehouse & Leonard Gross		
Total Fitness	£1.95	☐
Maximum Performance	£1.50	☐
Constance Mellor		
Guide to Natural Health	£1.25	☐
Natural Remedies for Common Ailments	£1.95	☐
Sonya Richmond		
Yoga and Your Health	£1.25	☐
Phyllis Speight		
Homoeopathy	£1.50	☐
Kenneth Lysons		
How to Cope with Hearing Loss	95p	☐
Dr Richard B Stuart		
Act Thin, Stay Thin	£1.50	☐
Dr Carl C Pfeiffer & Jane Banks		
Total Nutrition	£1.50	☐
Dr Hamilton Hall		
Be Your Own Back Doctor	£1.95	☐
José Silva and Michael Miele		
The Silva Mind Control Method	£2.50	☐
Dr Peter M Miller		
The Change Your Metabolism Diet	£1.95	☐
Slimming Magazine		
30-Day Formula	£3.95	☐

To order direct from the publisher just tick the titles you want
and fill in the order form.

Sports and activities handbooks now available in Panther Books

Pat Davis
Badminton Complete (illustrated) £1.25 ☐

Bruce Tegner
Karate (illustrated) £1.50 ☐

Bruce Tulloh
The Complete Distance Runner (illustrated) £1.95 ☐

Meda Mander
How to Trace Your Ancestors (illustrated) £1.50 ☐

Tom Hopkins
How to Master the Art of Selling £2.50 ☐

William Prentice
How to Start a Successful Business £2.50 ☐

Susan Glascock
A Woman's Guide to Starting Her Own Business £2.50 ☐

Alfred Tack
Sell Your Way to Success £1.25 ☐

Andrew Pennycook
The Book of Card Games £3.95 ☐

C Lukács and E Tarjan
Mathematical Games £1.50 ☐

Gyles Brandreth
The Complete Puzzler £1.50 ☐

Patrick Duncan (ed.)
The Panther Crossword Compendium (Vols 1 and 2) £1.95 ☐
each
Quizwords 1 £1.50 ☐
Quizwords 2 £1.50 ☐

To order direct from the publisher just tick the titles you want
and fill in the order form.

Titles of General Interest now available in Panther Books

Malcolm MacPherson (Editor)
The Black Box: Cockpit Voice Recorder
  Accounts of Nineteen Air Accidents   £1.95 ☐

Isaac Asimov
Asimov on Science Fiction   £2.50 ☐

Roy Harley Lewis
The Browser's Guide to Erotica   £1.95 ☐

Charles Berlitz
Native Tongues   £2.50 ☐

Carole Boyer
Names for Boys and Girls   £1.25 ☐

José Silva and Michael Miele
The Silva Mind Control Method   £2.50 ☐

Millard Arnold (editor)
The Testimony of Steve Biko   £2.50 ☐

John Howard Griffin
Black Like Me   £1.95 ☐

Desmond Morris
The Naked Ape   £1.95 ☐
The Pocket Guide to Man Watching   £2.95 ☐

Ivan Tyrell
The Survival Option   £2.50 ☐

Peter Laurie
Beneath the City Streets   £2.50 ☐

To order direct from the publisher just tick the titles you want
and fill in the order form.

All these books are available at your local bookshop or newsagent, or can be ordered direct from the publisher.

To order direct from the publisher just tick the titles you want and fill in the form below.

Name_____

Address _____

_____

Send to:
Panther Cash Sales
PO Box 11, Falmouth, Cornwall TR10 9EN.

Please enclose remittance to the value of the cover price plus:

UK 45p for the first book, 20p for the second book plus 14p per copy for each additional book ordered to a maximum charge of £1.63.

BFPO and Eire 45p for the first book, 20p for the second book plus 14p per copy for the next 7 books, thereafter 8p per book.

Overseas 75p for the first book and 21p for each additional book.

Panther Books reserve the right to show new retail prices on covers, which may differ from those previously advertised in the text or elsewhere.